THE PRINCI

THE PRINCIPLES OF POLICING

Michael S. Pike

Foreword by
the Rt. Hon. Lord Scarman, O.B.E.

First published 1985

Published by
THE MACMILLAN PRESS LTD
Houndmills, Basingstoke, Hampshire RG21 2XS
and London
Companies and representatives
throughout the world

Typeset by
Wessex Typesetters Ltd
Frome, Somerset

Printed in Hong Kong

British Library Cataloguing in Publication Data
Pike, Michael S.
The principles of policing.
1. Police—Great Britain
I. Title
363.2′0941   HV8195.A2
ISBN 0-333-38244-7
ISBN 0-333-38245-5 Pbk

Contents

Acknowledgements

The basis for this commentary on policing has been Lord Scarman's *Report on the Brixton Disorders*, together with the Royal Commission's *Report on Criminal Procedure*. Extracts from these reports and other Crown copyright material are reproduced with the kind permission of the Controller of Her Majesty's Stationery Office. These and other sources are acknowledged in the composite notes at the end of the book.

I should like to acknowledge the ready assistance given by the Commanding Officer and staff at the New York Police Academy. The social studies section of their initial training programme for recruits is the basis for much of the chapter on 'Sense and Sensitivity'.

For some other American sources, I am indebted to many of my friends and former colleagues at the John Jay College of Criminal Justice, New York. In particular, I am grateful to Professor P. J. Stead, formerly Dean of Academic Studies at the Police Staff College, Bramshill, and until 1983, Dean of Graduate Studies at John Jay College, whose advice and encouragement have been much appreciated.

MICHAEL S. PIKE

Foreword

by THE RT. HON LORD SCARMAN, O.B.E.

During the last few years police studies have come into their own as business of great social importance. It may be that the 1981 disorders in Brixton and Toxteth awoke the public conscience by the sheer surprise that such things could happen in the Britain of today.

Whatever the reason for the heightened interest in the principles and practice of policing, it is refreshing to find that not only academics and politicians but also policemen are concerned to analyse and reassess the role of the police in British society. Mr Pike's book is of absorbing interest and real value because the reader is able to appreciate the complex interaction of principle and practice. Practice modifies principle as surely as principle governs practice. The mark of the first-rate policeman is the ability to make not once but continually the correct decision when operational need appears to diverge from the requirements of principle. Here arises an important element in the policeman's discretion. Training, experience, intelligence, and character are the indispensable conditions for the proper exercise of his discretion, a word which is lawyers' jargon for the exercise of judgment in the particular circumstances of the case.

The year 1984 has posed new problems for the police in the maintenance of public order. They have had to handle the threat to public order arising from massed pickets at coal-mines and power-stations. The 1981 disorders were different in character; and perhaps a less serious threat than those of 1984 to the social acceptance of the strong arm of the police in the suppression of public disorder.

The police operations arising from the coal-strike will have to be studied and analysed. But the events of 1984 cannot be allowed to undermine the responsibility of the police to maintain public order, which includes the right of every one of us to move from one place to another without physical hindrance. It matters not whether those who would obstruct others in their use of the highway act upon the purest of motives or merely to do mischief; they must be restrained, if they cannot be persuaded to desist. The police problem, as ever, is to act effectively but in a way which is socially acceptable, and, of course, to keep scrupulously within the law.

Voices have been heard to query whether the police have any role in an industrial dispute. The answer is that they have only if a criminal act or a breach of the peace is threatened or committed. Where that situation exists, the policeman has to intervene. The real difficulty is as to the nature and scale of his intervention. In meeting that difficulty the policeman must exercise his own independent judgment, taking care to act within the law.

Studies such as the present work assist the police to make correct decisions and the public to understand their problem. I commend this book as helpful in the search, which is never-ending, for the correct balance between effective and socially acceptable policing. If it be true that policing cannot be effective in a free society unless it is socially acceptable, then the question arises how best to ensure that the public understand what is required of them to enable the police to act effectively. There is a duty on all of us to support the police, as there is a duty upon the police to ensure that they act in a way which commands the confidence of the community which they serve. The present work makes a substantial contribution to a better understanding by police and public of what is required of each other.

Introduction

Policing has always been a subject of interest to the public and rightly so, for the police hold a unique position in society. No other agency has such a capacity for influencing the lives of so many people from day to day and it is a reflection on the value of the police that, despite their task of regulating and controlling individual freedom, they are still held in high regard by the majority of the public. The British police and their capacity for controlling incidents of disorder without resorting to extreme measures of control have been the envy of the world and they have been regarded as a model on which policing in a democracy can be based.

In 1981, I had the privilege of representing the Police Staff College, Bramshill, as visiting lecturer at the John Jay College of Criminal Justice at the City University, New York. During the course of lecturing on comparative police systems, I had projected the British police system as an effective compromise between the centralised systems of policing found on the continent and the local and decentralised systems found in the United States. While extolling the virtues of the British system, the scenes of disorder at Brixton appeared on American television and these prompted questions from my students which had no immediate answer.

During research into certain aspects of American policing, it became clear that as a result of their own urban disturbances and race riots some years previously, they had adjusted policing methods and policies and, in particular, had introduced into their training programmes a wide range of social studies, with the objective of increasing an officer's social and human awareness. It was this social factor which had never previously featured in British police training. It formed the basis by which an officer could understand his role in society and how to perform his duties effectively.

Here was an indication of the professionalism found in many urban and other police departments in the United States, a professionalism whereby an officer understands the origins of his profession and the role of that profession in society.

Lord Scarman's Report on the Brixton Disorders proved to be a consolidation of many of the aspects of policing I had encountered in American police training programmes and this, together with the Report of the Royal Commission on Criminal Procedure, provided a comprehensive basis for a further analysis of the policing function. The result has been this attempt to examine the principles of policing. It is essentially a post-Scarman commentary on policing which draws on a variety of sources, old and new, in order to identify those underlying principles which have stood the test of time and shaped the modern police service.

The work involved has been a personal commitment prompted by the opportunity to increase my own professional knowledge and awareness by lecturing and research in the United States. It represents a modest contribution to the continuing dialogue between the police and the public which Lord Scarman hoped would follow his report. To this extent, the book is intended for the public in order that they can increase their understanding of the traditional nature of policing and the complexities of the police role. It is also hoped that police officers may find it a useful work of reference and the basis for a greater understanding of their profession.

Much of the comment and discussion is not original and sources are acknowledged where necessary. Where my own comments and observations are included, it is emphasised that they do not necessarily represent the views of any particular police force or the police service in general.

Author's Note
Any reference to a police officer in the text naturally includes a woman officer and any reference to 'he', 'him' and 'his' should be read accordingly.

M.S.P.

1 The Search for Principles

A search for principles of policing must necessarily involve an examination of the historical basis of the modern police system. 'The police are the public and the public are the police' aptly describes the collective responsibility for law and order which existed in Anglo-Saxon times. A crime was regarded as an act *contra pacem Domini*[1] and was not merely a crime against the victim but also a crime against the whole community. The responsibility for 'keeping the peace'[2] was placed firmly on the male population and this prompted a mutual participation by all the citizens.

This responsibility was reinforced by a system of mutual pledging whereby the King guaranteed his subjects a state of peace and security in return for their pledge of allegiance and good conduct. The state of peace guaranteed by the King was in reality a guarantee against external influence but the notion of the 'King's peace', fictionally extended to the whole realm, referred to the internal state of society and any criminal act could be regarded as an offence against the peace. Communities were structured into 'tythings',[3] 'hundreds'[4] and 'shires'[5] and the authority of the King extended through the 'shire-reeves'[6] who were responsible for law and order in each county.

This system of policing proved effective and was to survive the Norman Conquest. It proved adaptable to the feudal system and the functions of the sheriff were to a certain extent usurped by the feudal barons. The shire courts were supplemented by courts leet or manor courts. One of the officers appointed by the manor court was the 'comes-stabuli'[7] from which the word constable is derived and the 'constable' gradually assumed the function of the tythingman who was formerly in control of a tything. Under Henry II (1154–89), the system of mutual pledging was revived and every freeman was required to bear arms for the purpose of preserving the peace and pursuing criminals. The local responsibility for law and order became vested in the 'headborough'[8] who had to raise the hue and cry and every man was then obliged to

1

arm himself and join the chase. These measures were reflected in
the Statute of Winchester in 1285 whereby Edward I provided a
system of policing for both town and country based on local
participation. The sheriffs were responsible for raising the hue
and cry and every man between 15 and 60 had to possess arms in
readiness for use in keeping the peace. A system of 'watch and
ward' was established in towns which required the gates of the
town to be closed during the night and a watch established
according to population.

The Justice of the Peace Act in 1361 established the office of
justice of the peace and provided that, 'In every county in
England shall be assigned for the keeping of the Peace . . . three or
four of the most worthy in the county . . . to restrain offenders and
rioters and to arrest, take and chastise them . . . according to the
law and customs of the Realm.' They were appointed to assist the
sheriffs and the justices were assisted by the constables who
gradually assumed the role of enquiring into offences and
arresting offenders. This pattern of keeping the peace with its
relationship between the justice of the peace and constable was to
reaffirm the principle of local responsibility for law and order.
Although it proved incapable of containing the increasing crime
in cities and towns after the Industrial Revolution, it was clearly
adopted by Sir Robert Peel when establishing the Metropolitan
Police in 1829.

This principle of local responsibility survived a critical phase
during the eighteenth century. By the beginning of that century,
the country had witnessed the final breakdown of the feudal
system. The effects of the Industrial Revolution had produced an
urban society in which crime and disorder went virtually
unchecked. It is difficult to appreciate the extent of the problems
created by the mass movement of the population into the urban
areas. Drunkenness and poverty were commonplace and cities
such as London were unable to cope with the increasing demand
for housing and employment. Contemporary accounts refer to the
streets of London swarming with armed gangs, thieves and
pickpockets. The mob[9] were easily roused. On the approach roads
to London, robberies increased at an alarming rate. Whatever the
achievements had been in the industrial field, the first half of the
eighteenth century represented a complete breakdown of law and
order.

The only forces available to deal with these problems were the justices of the peace supported by the constables and watchmen. The effects of urbanisation, however, and the increase in commerce and trade had resulted in widespread corruption and bribery in pursuit of office. In such a climate, the justice of the peace or magistrate had little standing in the community. They received no salaries and survived mainly on fees. Courts were often held in taverns and business premises and the term 'trading justices' was widely used to describe their interest in fees rather than justice.

Constables and watchmen were similarly unpaid and although the constable was appointed to his office, the onerous nature of his duties often resulted in persons being paid to act on his behalf. These persons were invariably old or infirm and quite incapable of performing their proper function. Similarly, the watchmen would pay others to act for them and this process of substitution resulted in the most weak and feeble being employed. Neither the constables nor watchmen were capable of dealing with the armed gangs which roamed freely and it is difficult to understand why such an inefficient combination of justices and constables should have been so attractive during the subsequent debates leading to the reform of the policing system.

The impetus for reform was initiated by Henry Fielding who was appointed Chief Magistrate at Bow Street in 1748. Already a well-established author and writer, his *'Enquiry into the Causes of the Late Increase of Robbers'*, published in 1751 identified the cause as social emulation. He was very concerned about the effects of the growth in population, the slums, the excessive drinking and gambling and commented,

> The introduction of trade . . . hath indeed given a new face to the whole nation . . . and hath almost totally changed the manners, customs and habits of the people, more especially of the lower sort. The narrowness of their fortune is changed into wealth; the simplicity of their manners into craft; their frugality into luxury; their humility into pride, and their subjection into equality.

It was soon clear that Henry Fielding was to be no ordinary magistrate and he embarked on a course of action which was designed to enhance the status of magistrates and provide a more effective force to patrol the streets. The partnership between the magistracy and the constables was consciously retained and although his efforts to reform the magistracy were largely frustrated by the justices' corrupt involvement with licensing and gambling establishments, his selection of several parish constables to assist him in arresting criminal gangs proved highly successful.

These constables were essentially 'thief-takers' who were motivated by fees since the law encouraged rewards for persons who assisted in the arrest and conviction of felons. Henry Fielding sought to awaken the public interest in crime and the public were encouraged to report details of all crimes and criminals. The emergence of a separate force of 'thief-takers' known as 'Mr Fielding's People' had demonstrated to the public that the unacceptable level of crime could be reduced. In 1754, Henry Fielding was succeeded by his half-brother, John, who continued the efforts against crime with some financial support from the government. Further experiments in policing continued but there was little enthusiasm or support for any large scale extension of patrols. Nevertheless, the 'Bow Street Runners' had achieved a wide reputation and their services were often called upon outside London. Details of crimes and wanted persons were also being distributed outside London and John Fielding continued to urge for reform and the establishment of more horse patrols in and around the capital.

The government's hesitancy was understandable since although they recognised that law and order was their responsibility, they were reluctant to be seen as providing any force which could be regarded by the public as a dreaded 'arm of government'. In 1761, they rejected a request by John Fielding to use the military in connection with some dangerous criminals wanted for robbery. By 1763, horse patrols had been established on the highways around London but the Government felt disinclined to finance these patrols and insisted that the cost should be borne by the surrounding counties. This was an attempt to place the responsibility for policing areas outside the capital on the local counties and boroughs and was a reaffirmation of the principle of local responsibility. A further plan by John Fielding to place all constables and watchmen in Westminster under the direction of the chief magistrate was a renewal of the established role of the justices for keeping the peace.

It would be easy to conclude, in the light of later developments in the early part of the nineteenth century, that the contribution made by Henry and John Fielding was not a significant one, but it was from their office in Bow Street that the first efforts were made to establish a special body of police. They recognised that the old system of voluntary watchmen and constables was insufficient to meet the wider demands and problems of an expanding urban population.[10]

There can be no doubt that the impetus gained by their innovative approach was not lost after John Fielding's death in 1780. The 'Gordon Riots' of that year prompted the introduction of the London and Westminster Police Bill by Pitt's Government which proposed a police force for London with paid officers responsible to a commissioner. The proposed system incorporated the parish constables and watchmen but was widely opposed and was rejected by Parliament. The bill was ahead of its time and the public were not yet ready to accept such a system. The political and constitutional arguments were to continue for another thirty years but at Bow Street further practical measures were being adopted.

In 1790, the chief magistrate, Sir Sampson Wright, set up a small force to patrol the streets of London from his office. They were under his direct control and could be sent to any incident at his discretion. The Middlesex Justices Act of 1792 created new magistrates' offices to work in conjunction with Bow Street. This provided an opportunity for further constables to operate from each office and they were given increased powers. The act was intended to prevent corruption among the magistracy and police courts were established on the Bow Street model. Provision was made for constables and magistrates to be paid from central funds.

One of the new justices appointed was Patrick Colquhoun, a man of some vision, who acknowledged the achievements of Henry and John Fielding. His contribution in the literary field was significant and he advocated many social measures to alleviate the distress and suffering of the poor. His social awareness and sense of responsibility were reflected in the way he defined the function of the police and the value he attached to the office of constable which he asserted was 'as old as the monarchy'.

Colquhoun's radical views are probably best illustrated by his celebrated *Treatise on the Police of the Metropolis* in which he advocated a scientific approach to policing and commented, 'Police in this Country may be considered as a new science; the properties of which consist not in the Judicial powers that lead to punishment, and which belong to Magistrates alone; but in the Prevention and Detection of Crimes, and in those other functions which relate to Internal Regulations for the well ordering and comfort of Civil Society.'[11]

Colquhoun did not seek to abolish the traditional partnership of magistrate and constable and noted obvious advantages of local control but his main concern was to establish an effective police system in London controlled by a 'general superintendance' so that the combined energies of the parish constables, deputy constables, water patrol and Bow Street officers could be channelled in the right direction. On a wider scale, he advocated a national system of policing under the direction of a 'Central Board of Police Revenue' which would be financed by licensing a variety of general traders such as pedlars, pawnbrokers and second-hand dealers. He envisaged a central supervisory role over the enforcement of the law and the collection of records relating to offences.

This board would consist of commissioners who would collate details of crime throughout the country on behalf of the government 'where it will be accurately discovered whether it increases or diminishes'. This was the first notion of an annual report and a national view of criminality for the benefit of Parliament. He suggested a national framework of selected magistrates who would control all the constables in their respective areas, with petty constables being supervised by high constables. He urged the establishment of 'a well-regulated and energetic Police, conducted with purity, zeal and intelligence.' His concept of a centrally controlled police system was based on his firm belief that the prevention of crime was the primary object of police.[12]

Colquhoun supported his belief in prevention by commenting on the serious threat to personal liberty which was his justification for advocating a proper system of policing.

> In vain do we boast of those liberties which are our birthright if the vilest and most depraved . . . deprive us of the privilege of travelling upon the highways . . . without risk of being assaulted or robbed; and perhaps wounded or murdered. In vain may we boast of the security which our Laws afford us, if we cannot lie down to rest in our habitations without the dread

of a burglary being committed, our property invaded, and our lives exposed to imminent danger before the approach of morning.[13]

His remedy was forcibly expressed:

Let it once become the duty of one body of men to charge themselves with the execution of the laws for the prevention of crimes, and the detection of offences – let them be armed with proper and apposite powers for that purpose and the state of Society will speedily become ameliorated and improved; a greater degree of security will be extended to the peaceful subject, and the blessings of civil liberty will be enlarged.[14]

It is perhaps significant that Colquhoun viewed the police as the protectors of civil liberty in contrast to some modern commentators who distort the police function as being a threat to civil liberties. Such is the present lack of understanding of the police role in society.

Liberty was a sensitive issue at the time of Colquhoun. 1776 had seen a revolution in America, followed by another in France in 1789. The experience of France after the Revolution which had resulted in a strong centralised police system was a powerful influence on the minds of English politicians. In 1798, Colquhoun had put forward his scheme of policing to a Select Committee of the House of Commons yet his proposals for a national police system were rejected. Like the London and Westminster Police Bill in 1785, it never reached the statute book.

Colquhoun had also written a *Treatise on the Commerce and Police of the River Thames* and in June 1798 a force of Marine Police was formed to deal with the 'acts of peculation, fraud, embezzlement, pillage and depredation, through the medium of the various and numerous classes of depraved characters who are employed upon the River, seeking for opportunities to acquire plunder and who . . . are only to be restrained and overawed by an apposite River Police, exclusively directed to that object alone, and aided by a competent civil force'.[15]

Colquhoun had recognised that criminal activity on the river could be prevented and, supported by John Harriott who took over the operational direction, he organised the structure of the new marine police. Its impact was immediate and its success remarkable. Within twelve months the river had been cleared of its worst criminal element and the effectiveness of a preventive force had been ably demonstrated. It had been established to combat the considerable loss to the shipping interests on the river which were estimated to be losing some half a million pounds each year. The value of goods stolen decreased by 80–90 per cent. The shipping merchants who had largely financed the scheme saw their profits enhanced and the government also benefited by the consequential increase in revenue.

Colquhoun's efforts at police reform should have been strengthened by the success of the marine police but there was little response from government and general public apathy. Radzinowicz, in commenting on the failure of the Police Bill of 1785, said: '. . . the idea had been abandoned and never revived, even when the remarkable success of the Thames River Police had given so tangible an illustration of what a preventive civil force could achieve. The public acceptance that nothing more could or should be done had become almost a settled habit of mind'.[16]

There is little doubt that Colquhoun's contribution to the theory and principles of policing provided an important link between the progress made by Henry and John Fielding and the later reforms. Many of his ideas were adopted by Sir Robert Peel when establishing the Metropolitan Police in 1829. He had demonstrated the effectiveness of prevention and his 'Science of Preventive Policing' advocated that police powers should be based, 'upon the broad scale of General Prevention – mild in its operation – effective in its results; having justice and humanity for its basis, and the general security of the State and Individuals for its ultimate object'.[17]

The value of prevention by increased patrols was being recognised elsewhere and in 1800, Sir Richard Ford, the Chief Magistrate at Bow Street, re-established the mounted patrols which had proved so effective. These new patrols were armed and wore distinctive uniforms. They had full powers of pursuit in and around the capital and their presence did much to reassure coach travellers and to contain the incidents of robbery. The early years of the nineteenth century saw further efforts to establish an organised system of policing but despite the clear evidence of its effectiveness, opposition remained.

Later developments and the establishment of the Metropolitan Police are well chronicled elsewhere[18] but it seems clear that social and industrial unrest, resulting in disorder and riots, were instrumental in forcing the issue. In 1812, an army of 12 000 had been deployed in the North and Midlands in an effort to suppress the machine-wrecking activities of the Luddites, a group of workers who had rioted against low wages and unemployment attributed to the introduction of textile-making machines. The army eventually succeeded in suppressing the riots but only at the cost of extreme hostility and bitterness against the army and the government.

In 1819, against a background of social tension, a large demonstration took place in St Peter's Field, Manchester, primarily aimed at petitioning for parliamentary reform. Riots broke out and although the rioters were dispersed by yeomanry and hussars, eleven people were killed. The incident was publicised as the 'Peterloo Massacres' and the message was clear. Unless the angry working classes could be subdued by force, the whole fabric of society was threatened and anarchy would ensue. It was clear that the use of force was abhorrent to the ordinary people and informed opinion began to support those who were advocating an organised system of policing throughout the country.

The empirical nature of policing developed by the Fieldings at Bow Street together with the more scientific approach adopted with such success by Colquhoun had provided a firm basis for reform. It was left to Sir Robert Peel, as Home Secretary, to cultivate public opinion as to the merits of an efficient system of police. Peel, influenced by the utilitarianism of Jeremy Bentham[19] and other social philosophies, was sensitive to the objection that principles of liberty might be eroded and his task of influencing Parliament was a considerable one. The problem which had to be overcome was essentially a simple one. How could he impose a system of policing on a public which historically had rejected any notion of organised force as being inconsistent with individual liberty. The irreconcilable views were clearly identified by the Select Committee on the Police of the Metropolis when publishing their report in 1822.

> . . . It is difficult to reconcile an effective system of police, with that perfect freedom of action and exemption from interference, which are the great privileges and blessings of society in this country; and your Committee think that the forfeiture or

curtailment of such advantages would be too great a sacrifice for improvements in police or facilities in detection of crime, however desirable in themselves if abstractly considered.[20]

This view, reinforced by accounts from Europe of the rigours of a centralised police system, reflected the fear that traditional British liberties would be threatened. The establishment of a police system would be seen as an unwarranted extension of government power and it was clear to Sir Robert Peel that the best way to overcome opposition was to present his proposals for a police system as an extension of existing institutions. The new force was not to be seen as an arm of Government but would be local in character and the relationship of magistrate and constable would be preserved.

Colquhoun's principle of prevention of crime rather than punishment was a further ingredient since prevention implied a passive presence on the streets rather than an aggressive force which might alienate the public. Consequently, the 'new police' were to be unarmed and, in addressing Parliament, Peel said that he intended 'to proceed slowly with the experiment with a cautious feeling of the way and deriving aid from experience'. The emphasis was on a 'police service' rather than a 'force' and there was a clear intention at the outset to win public approval. The first instructions drawn up for the Metropolitan Police in 1829 embodied this new philosophy of policing which has character-ised the British police service ever since.

> He will be civil and obliging to all people of every rank and class. He must be particularly cautious not to interfere idly or unnecessarily in order to make a display of his authority; when required to act, he will do so with decision and boldness; on all occasions he may expect to receive the fullest support in the proper exercise of his authority. He must remember that there is no qualification so indispensable to a police-officer as a perfect command of temper, never suffering himself to be moved in the slightest degree by any language or threats that may be used; if he does his duty in a quiet and determined manner, such conduct will probably excite the well-disposed of the by-standers to assist him, if he requires them.

Peel entrusted the leadership of the new force to Richard

Mayne, a lawyer, and Charles Rowan, a soldier. The latter is generally regarded as having made the greater contribution in organising the force and basing it on military lines. There is little doubt they were greatly assisted in their task by the fact that Peel, in steering the Act through Parliament, had left many details of the new police system open so that the two commissioners had considerable discretion in deciding on policy and organisation. Early hostility to the new force was soon overcome and much credit is due to Rowan and Mayne in adopting a flexible approach and learning through experience.

In retrospect, it is possible to identify several factors which enabled the new police system to survive the early period of hostility. Firstly, the traditional roles of the constable and magistrate were embodied in the system. The power and function of the constable were retained and supplemented by the new philosophy of crime prevention. In determining the objects of the new force in 1829, Mayne said:

> The primary object of an efficient police is the prevention of crime; the next that of detection and punishment of offenders if crime is committed. To these ends all the efforts of Police must be directed. The protection of life and property, the preservation of public tranquility, and the absence of crime, will alone prove whether those efforts have been successful, and whether the objects for which the Police were appointed have been attained.[21]

Justices of the Peace had for centuries been responsible for preserving the peace and by appointing Rowan and Mayne as magistrates, Parliament was able to retain the historical subordination of the constable to the justice as a method of control which was remote from Government. Despite this, the constitutional position of the new police was blurred by the fact that the Home Secretary exercised direct control over the two commissioners and was responsible to Parliament for their actions. The county and borough police forces which were formed later were not fettered by any central control but were clearly under the direction of the local justices. Since justices have a judicial function, the old constitutional doctrine of the 'separation of powers'[22] seems to have been ignored.

This doctrine asserted that liberty depended on the executive, judicial and legislative functions of government being separate. The control exercised by the Home Secretary and the justices over the police was a constitutional objection which does not appear to have been forcibly argued then or since.

There seems little doubt that any constitutional objection was swallowed up by the fact that the constables retained their old common law powers and were subject to the same laws as the ordinary citizen. A Royal Commission set up in 1836 to enquire as to the best method of establishing efficient county police forces in England and Wales concluded that, 'The chief and proper objection to the police forces abroad are that they act on powers which are arbitrary; the force we propose can only act on powers which are legal and for which they will be responsible to the courts of law and ultimately to Parliament.' As recently as 1962, a Royal Commission reiterated the same principle that 'British liberty does not depend on dispersal of police power but on the supremacy of Parliament and the rule of law.'

A further principle which characterised the new police service was that the constables were independent with regard to enforcing the law yet still accountable to a democratically elected Parliament through the Home Secretary. Complaints were effectively dealt with and it was soon realised that the emphasis on courtesy and impartiality was a unique feature of the new system. *The Times* was able to report in 1830 that, 'We have seen nothing but exemplary courtesy, forbearance and propriety, great willingness to act and, when occasion calls for it, to refrain from acting.'

The unqualified success of the Metropolitan Police in the years following 1829 soon provided a platform for further reforms. Although the government had left policing outside of London to local discretion, serious public disorder in 1831 over the Reform Bill required urgent action. Riots occurred in Bristol, Nottingham, Exeter, Coventry and other cities and it was left to the watchmen and constables to try and contain the situation. Parliament responded by a hastily contrived Special Constables Act of 1831 which provided for justices to conscript men on the occasion of riot or threatened riot.

It would have been a comparatively easy exercise to adopt a system of policing for the whole country based on the Metropolitan model but the government were reluctant to respond in too radical a way. They appointed a Royal Commission to report on municipal corporations and, as an interim measure, passed an act whereby a rate could be levied from each parish to pay for watchmen and street patrols. It seemed clear that central government was not inclined to finance the provision of a police force for areas outside of London. They could justify the setting up of the Metropolitan Police since London was the seat of government and the nation's capital but they adhered to the principle that there was a local responsibility for law and order.

The Municipal Corporations Act of 1835 required town councils to be established in each of the 178 boroughs in England and Wales which up until then had been granted royal charters. The Act provided for the setting up of Watch Committees who were required to 'appoint a sufficient number of fit men' to be sworn in as constables to preserve the peace and prevent robberies. The common law powers of the constable were retained but too much was left to the discretion of individual boroughs. Some responded to the challenge and established efficient forces based on the conditions and regulations of the Metropolitan Police but others seemed quite content to perpetuate the existing structure of part-time constables and fee-earners. Many boroughs realised they could fulfil their obligations under the act without recourse to any measures which might prove costly. There were no criteria for establishments so that the act also provided for the appointment of special constables if the regular officers were unable to maintain law and order. The act was significant, however, in that the foundation had been laid for subsequent reform which was to witness the extension of police forces to the county areas of England and Wales.

A Royal Commission in 1836 was appointed to examine the best means of establishing efficient police forces in the county areas and their conclusions challenged the suitability of the magistracy to control and maintain local police forces. The Commission concluded that the magistrates were too remote from the working class and did not fully understand the problems associated with policing. It was felt that the magistrates, who were on the whole wealthy, were often guided by self-interest but the most significant conclusion touched on the constitutional principle that the judicial and executive functions of the magistrates were incompatible and should be quite distinct.

Nevertheless, the subsequent County Police Act of 1839 still provided for the justices in Quarter Sessions to establish a police force in their county area but, being permissive only, many counties failed to make use of the act. This was largely due to the financial implications but some resistance was still based on the threat to individual liberty which had dominated and dogged the reform movement at the end of the eighteenth century. Nottingham, for example, based their objection on the grounds of expense and still held the view that a police force might be used for the purposes of arbitrary aggression upon the liberties of the people. Even in Lord Palmerston's adopted town of Romsey, an attempt to amalgamate the borough police with Hampshire provoked a strong reaction from local traders who feared a loss of livelihood and liberty at the hands of the county police.

A Select Committee in 1853 noted that 13 boroughs had still not established any police force under the enabling Act of 1835 and only half of the 56 counties had responded to the County Police Act 1839. The Committee concluded that the fragmented organisation frustrated any reform and that there was a clear conflict between towns and counties over jurisdiction. There was evidence that where police forces had been established, crime had decreased and the government recognised the long-term advantages of consolidating the county and borough forces.

The path of reform right through to the Police Act 1964 was a difficult one. Early attempts to introduce a consolidating Bill were frustrated by the boroughs who resisted the proposed restrictions and shift of power from the Watch Committees to the rural justices. The government were determined to urge reform and recognised that the fragmented system of policing must be placed on a proper footing with central supervision from the Home Office. The struggle to wrest control from small, inefficient borough forces was to dominate subsequent reform.

The effect of the Crimea War in 1854 led to military detachments being withdrawn from various strategic areas of the country and the reluctance of smaller boroughs to respond to a Government request to establish adequate police forces led to the introduction of a Bill which was designed to establish the principle of central supervision and reconcile it with the former principle of local responsibility for law and order.

The measures contained in the County and Borough Police Act of 1856 included the appointment of three Inspectors of Constabulary. Their function was to submit annual reports to Parliament and to assess the efficiency of police forces. Since the

Exchequer grant of one quarter of the cost of pay and clothing was made dependent on efficiency, the assessment of efficiency was essentially a value for money exercise. The Exchequer grant was denied to forces serving a population of less than 5000 and this proved an inducement for smaller forces to merge with others. Agreements to merge could only be revoked by the Home Secretary. The 1856 Act required counties to establish rural police forces where none existed and the county police were granted the same jurisdiction as borough officers.

The act caused widespread hostility particularly in the borough forces who regarded the imposition of an Inspectorate as degrading. The central theme of government supervision provoked a comparison with the strong centralised European forces. Nevertheless, the Inspectorate proved an excellent vehicle for reform since it operated independently from the Home Office and the Inspectors dealt directly with Chief Constables. They operated and lived in separate regions remote from Westminster and national policies began to emerge from their annual reports to the Home Secretary.

By 1860, there were 226 separate police forces ranging from the Metropolitan Police down to small borough forces with just one constable. The anomalies were highlighted by the Inspectorate who advocated that small forces should be abolished and that the Home Secretary should provide rules for borough forces in the same way as rules had been provided for the counties. In 1874, the Exchequer grant was increased from a quarter to one-half of the cost of pay and clothing and this provided an opportunity for the government to exercise a stronger influence and tighter control.

An Act of 1877 restricted the formation of new forces where the population was under 20 000 and the speed of reform can be measured by the fact that Palmerston's Bill, rejected in 1855, had provided that boroughs below 20 000 population should lose their independent forces. The real issue was the resistance by the watch committees to any transfer of power to the rural justices. If the proposal had been accepted in 1855, no less than 120 out of 180 boroughs would have been compelled to merge with other counties or boroughs. Such a drastic step was unacceptable to Parliament and the government realised it had underestimated the political strength of the boroughs. Even the 1877 Act did not apply to existing boroughs of under 20 000 population and other signs of resistance to central control were clearly evident.

The Home Office, sensing the delicate balance between central and local control of the police adopted a conscious policy of advice and guidance to police forces. 'Letters to police authorities should be free from taint of dictation or direction.' The Inspectorate was advised to approach local authorities direct and lead them in the right direction but with discretion. It was a similar exercise to Peel's 'cautious feeling of the way'. Sir William Harcourt, as Home Secretary, also added his weight in support of the local authorities. 'I cannot consent to the Procrustean rules of the Inspectors who are quite ignorant of the needs of the localities . . . against the local authorities who know their own affairs much better.'

This endorsement of local control failed to recognise the real conflict at local level. The Municipal Corporations Act of 1835 which had set up borough forces had provided Watch Committees with the power to make regulations to prevent the neglect or abuse of police duties and powers. They could also dismiss any constable who was negligent or unfit for office. Many Chief Constables in the borough forces clashed with their watch committees over these issues. The statutory power to make regulations restricted the chief officer's control of his force and many followed the independent policies of their colleagues in the county forces.

This local conflict persisted but the inefficiency of the small borough forces was apparent. The Local Government Act of 1888 abolished borough forces serving a population of under 10 000 but the provisions of the act, which reformed local government, were to have wider implications. The act established elected county councils and county borough councils with the result that the local justices of the peace ceased to maintain their absolute control over the police. Standing Joint Committees were set up in the counties consisting of equal numbers of justices and county councillors. The new democracy of county councils wanted greater control over the police and relied on the experience of the borough Watch Committees since 1835 to support their claim.

The traditional relationship between the police and the justices, however, was too entrenched to vanish overnight but the decline in the influence of the justices can be traced to the emergence of the standing joint committees. The joint membership of the committee was a compromise between the traditional principle that justices had a duty to preserve the peace and the democratic principle of accountability through elected representatives. The suitability of magistrates to maintain and control the police had long been questioned.[23] If central government had imposed an inspectorate to assess the cost effectiveness of police forces, it was hard to resist the parallel argument that local government should have a similar interest in the efficiency of police forces, which were financed in part from local rates.

The pattern for further reform had been set. In the county forces, the Chief Constable enjoyed greater control than the Chief Constable in the Borough forces who was in some cases subjected to the firmer control of the Watch Committee. The county Chief Constable's authority grew as the influence of the justices declined. He enjoyed a looser relationship with the Standing Joint Committee and this enabled the county forces to develop free of any rigid political influence. In the borough forces, however, the chief constable was to a large extent a 'puppet' of the local council. This may have enhanced accountability to elected councillors but in some cases, there were disquieting indications that true impartiality was being eroded.

The early part of the twentieth century was characterised by the reassessment of the role of the police in serious public disorder. A select committee in 1908 found that the army had assisted the police on no less than 24 occasions in the preceding 38 years in order to quell rioters. The committee had been set up following the Tonypandy Riots in South Wales and, in assessing the justification for using the army against the civilian population, they were stirring the ashes of dead controversies. The birth of the modern police service in 1829 was the culmination of a reform movement which had urged a civil force to maintain law and order and it was therefore hardly surprising that the committee should deplore the use of the military for such purposes. It is of interest that in the recommendations of this 1908 Committee we find the first notion of mutual aid between forces. It was recommended that the Home Secretary should have the power to require any county force to supply up to 10 per cent of its strength in order to assist any other area where law and order could not be maintained by local resources.

Events, however, were moving more quickly than the Select Committee. Further rioting occurred in South Wales in 1910 which necessitated the despatch of military reinforcements 'to act with the civil authorities as circumstances may require'. The

Home Secretary directed that the military were not to be used unless it was clear that police reinforcements were unable to cope. The following year, military detachments were sent to Liverpool to deal with industrial unrest and the army were also used in the famous Sidney Street siege in the same year during which three policemen were shot, although this latter incident can be distinguished on the grounds that the armed force was used against Russian anarchists and not the civilian population.

As the twentieth century progressed, the issue was consumed by the advent of war and the principle that the police were an unarmed civilian force with the responsibility to protect and not oppress the public was firmly re-established. There is little doubt that the First World War moulded the police service into a more unified body. Wars tend to result in national cohesion at all levels and the police service was no exception. This new-found unity provided new-found strength and the police, following the example of trade unions, began to demand improved conditions. The Home Office was indifferent to these representations and the police strike of 1918 was to provide the impetus for the setting up of the Desborough Committee and the birth of the Police Federation.

These were not merely milestones in police history. The government, not only concerned that the army might wish to follow the police example, recognised that the principle of an independent and impartial police service was at stake. Recent history had involved the police in many incidents of industrial unrest and the creation of a police union was seen as a threat to the preservation of law and order. A police union would be bound to sympathise with other unions against the government and in that situation the independence of the police would be in doubt.

The first report of the Desborough Committee was completed with commendable speed and the Police Act 1919 provided that police officers were not permitted to belong to a trade union and also provided for the establishment of an alternative representative body. The first Police Regulations were promulgated in 1920 and provided the basis for national conditions of service.

The second report included several recommendations designed to wrest further control from the watch committees in the borough forces and although the committee rejected the notion of a national police service, some recommendations reflected a greater measure of central control. A Police Department was to be set up in the Home Office, improved training methods were to be adopted and procedures introduced to facilitate co-operation between forces. At a local level, borough forces serving a population of under 50 000 were to be abolished and the power to appoint, promote and discipline police officers in the boroughs was to be transferred from the watch committee to the Chief Constable.

The opposition from the borough forces merely echoed the objections of the mid-nineteenth century. Many thought it was an adverse reflection on the capacity, integrity and loyalty of local authorities. The familiar conflict persisted between those who feared a more centralised system of policing and those who recognised that the merger of smaller forces was inevitable if a truly professional police service was to be established. The struggle of smaller forces to survive the mounting pressure was to continue right up to the Police Act of 1964 which was finally to reconcile the principle of local control with that of central supervision.

During the first part of the twentieth century, the police service was also subjected to closer scrutiny by a public who, while recognising the *raison d'être*, were beginning to question the scope of its function. The Royal Commission on Police Activities of 1906 was set up following suggestions of bribery and brutality. The Commission concluded that the Metropolitan Police, against whom the allegations had been made, discharged their duties with honesty, discretion and efficiency. They added, however, that occasional misconduct was naturally expected by every person conversant with experience of life. *The Times* somewhat optimistically commented that the Commission's report 'should put an end once and for all to these shameless and false attacks on the Police'.

Generally speaking, the police constable of the nineteenth century enjoyed popular support from the public but with the advent of the motor car, it was inevitable that the duty of enforcing a wide variety of regulatory traffic offences would not only bring the police officer into contact with a wider cross section of the public but would naturally provoke some hostility. It is not difficult to understand how popular support for the police was undermined by the task of enforcing unpopular laws against a section of the community which was basically law-abiding and would never consider themselves as criminals in the true sense.

Theories on the content of criminal law are developed later[24] but the public could be excused for thinking that acts of carelessness, forgetfulness or inexperience should attract other remedies rather than criminal sanctions. As the twentieth century progressed, the duties and powers of the constable increased as did the risk that over-zealous enforcement would alienate public opinion. An important principle was at stake – the principle of policing by consent which recognised the necessity for the police to win public approval of their actions.

The police enjoyed a high point of public approval during the General Strike of 1926. The early part of the century had been punctuated by violent clashes between various sections of the community, particularly those associated with the trade unions and suffragette movements. The climate of 1926 was a difficult one but the police acquitted themselves well and diffused many explosive situations involving organised labour. Their handling of public order incidents was firm and decisive and the public were impressed by the degree of restraint and control. There is little doubt that the rejection of a Police Union by the Desborough Committee and the statutory restriction on members of the police service being members of trade unions was fully vindicated. The police were able to adopt a fully impartial role and this did much to allay public anxiety and win approval for their actions. Public approval was so widespread that *The Times* launched a National Police Fund as an expression of national gratitude.

The fickle nature of popular support, however, was soon evident. Allegations of corruption and oppressiveness undermined the mutual confidence between the public and the police. The Royal Commission of 1929 considered this relationship and concluded, 'There is we believe, an instinctive and deep-rooted sympathy between the public and the police, which has never really been broken, in spite of minor misunderstandings and cases of friction which occasionally ruffle the relations between them.'[25] A later Royal Commission in 1960 arranged for a survey of public opinion to be undertaken which showed that 83 per cent of the public professed a great respect for the police. The Commission were able to conclude, 'We therefore assert confidently . . . that relations between the police and the public are on the whole very good, and we have no reason to suppose that they have ever, in recent times, been otherwise.'[26]

The early principle remains that the police can only operate with the consent and approval of the public. There is nothing subtle or difficult in recognising that this principle has been the key to the relative success of the police service in this country. The underlying fear in the late eighteenth century and early nineteenth century was that any organised police force would be under the control of central government and remote from the public. Consequently, the modern police service developed along a path which ensured that the police remained independent of political control. The path was a difficult one since a recurring criticism was the lack of accountability to local or central government.

The Royal Commission set up in 1960 under the chairmanship of Sir Henry Willink, considered *inter alia* the status and accountability of members and chief officers of police forces. A further consideration was the relationship of the police with the public and the means of ensuring that complaints by the public were being effectively dealt with. These two issues were very much related and the subsequent Police Act of 1964 recognised the tripartite nature of effective police arrangements. Effectiveness includes the accountability of the police service and the manner in which complaints are investigated. The act set out the responsibilities and powers of chief constables, police authorities and the Secretary of State and this acknowledged the professional expertise, the interest of the local community and the national interest.

Among the functions of a chief constable included in the 1964 Act are the direction and control of his police force and it is widely acknowledged that chief constables should be operationally independent. This is not to say, however, that the influence of police authorities and the Home Office is not important in formulating policies but there is a considerable difference between influence and interference. Police authorities and the Home Secretary were given statutory functions to maintain and promote respectively the efficiency of police forces. The functions of a police authority were also subjected to close scrutiny by the Home Secretary but the act provided for a collective control of the police service in such a way that a chief constable found himself accountable not only to the law, but to local police authorities and the Home Secretary.

It is difficult to extract from this historical account of the development of the police service those principles of policing which have survived the difficult path of reform but the traditional common law role of the constable, faithfully retained by the first Commissioners of the Metropolitan Police, was a basis for the development of a service which set out to win public confidence and acceptability. There is no better commentary on policing with public approval than this extract from the original instructions to the Metropolitan Police in 1829.

> . . . much depends on the approval and co-operation of the public, and these have always been determined by the degree of the esteem and respect in which the Police are held. Therefore, every member of the force must remember that it is his duty to protect and help members of the public, no less than to bring offenders to justice. Consequently, while prompt to prevent crime and arrest criminals, he must look on himself as the servant and guardian of the general public and treat all law-abiding citizens, irrespective of their race, colour, creed or social position, with unfailing patience and courtesy.

It is a measure of the wisdom and foresight of the first Commissioners that the nature of policing in this country was moulded in such a way that policing by consent has remained a basic principle ever since. The Commissioners recognised the importance of the common law role of the constable which itself had developed from the earliest principle of local responsibility for law and order. By emphasising the need for public approval and co-operation, the Commissioners also embodied another early principle that there should be a collective responsibility to maintain law and order.

The new system of police which emerged in 1829, therefore, was already calculated to attract public support by being a continuation of the existing system but it was the emerging principle of prevention, coupled with the principle of minimum force, which gave the new police its unique qualities.

Once established, public approval and respect had not only to be earned but retained. This is as relevant today as it ever was and there are three important areas of police conduct which are crucial to the principle of policing by consent. These are police ethics, police discretion and sensitive policing. These three topics are enlarged upon in later chapters but their importance lies in the fact that they relate to the whole field of police conduct. The police are not responsible for the laws they have to enforce but they are responsible for ensuring that the degree and balance of enforcement is in tune with public opinion and public expectations.

The independence of the police from political or other control, though not totally accepted, is nevertheless well established but this independence does not give the police the right to act irresponsibly. They are accountable in many ways and it has already been stressed that one of the most important regulating factors is that the police must secure public approval for their actions.

It is, therefore, not surprising that when Lord Scarman conducted his enquiry into the Brixton Disorders in 1981 he should refer to 'two well-known principles of policing a free society'. He referred to them as 'consent and balance' and 'independence and accountability'.[27] The events at Brixton in 1981 raised serious questions as to the nature of policing and it is important to examine these events more closely if these two principles are to be fully understood.

2 Brixton – a Re-Statement of Principles

One of the two principles of policing identified by Lord Scarman in his Report on the Brixton Disorders,[1] namely, 'consent and balance', must be viewed in the context of policing generally but it will assist an understanding of this principle if we examine the conclusions reached by Lord Scarman and the evidence on which these conclusions were based.

With the passing of time, it is easy to forget the serious nature of the disorders which occurred at Brixton in April 1981. On the evening of Saturday, 11 April, alone, 279 police officers were injured, at least 45 members of the public were injured, a large number of police and other vehicles were destroyed or damaged (some by fire) and 28 buildings were damaged or destroyed by fire. With police resources fully engaged in dispersing the rioters, widespread looting occurred.[2]

Lord Scarman, addressing the House of Lords, almost a year after the disturbances, emphasised the seriousness of the situation and the need for a strong and well-supported police force.

> If that thin blue line had been overwhelmed, and it nearly was on that Saturday night, there is no other way of dealing with it except the awful ultimate requirement of calling the Army. To turn the military inwards on British people is not something which our tolerant and free society can possibly accept.

He went on to refer to Northern Ireland and the disastrous withdrawal of the Royal Ulster Constabulary from the policing role following the intervention of the Army in 1969. This had shown that unless the police were not only strong but well supported by the people, they might find themselves in that sort of situation which was the beginning of the end of liberty and a tolerant society.

In his Report analysing the causes of the disturbances, Lord Scarman rightly identified a variety of political, social and economic reasons. He also noted major criticisms of the police, namely, racial prejudice, harassment, unimaginative and inflexible policing, over-reaction to the disorders, delay and lack of vigour in handling the disorders, and the failure to act against looting.[3]

The first three criticisms were offered as an underlying cause of the disorders in that over a period of time they had resulted in a serious breakdown in relations between the police and the community. This in turn led to a loss of confidence in the police and increased the hostility of young blacks towards the police. The last three criticisms from the evidence before Lord Scarman referred to matters arising during the disorders and have no relevance to the general deterioration of mutual trust and confidence beforehand. They are relevant, however, in examining public order and the police role.[4]

In summarising the evidence of racial prejudice, Lord Scarman concluded that it did manifest itself occasionally in the behaviour of a few officers on the streets who wrongly assumed that all young black people are potential criminals. He ruled out any suggestion that racial bias was to be found amongst senior police officers. It would not be surprising to the ordinary citizen to find that a police service which is a reflection of the society it serves does have amongst its members a few officers who are inclined towards racial prejudice but Lord Scarman rejects this on the basis that the police must have higher standards than those in the rest of society.[5]

Lord Scarman saw the solution in imposing a closer scrutiny on candidates for the service and there is clearly some scope for a far more comprehensive assessment of recruits. Many American forces require candidates to undergo psychiatric and psychological screening before being accepted and it is suggested that elements of racial prejudice can be identified by specific tests as well as other traits which might render a person unsuitable for appointment. It is, however, a difficult area since the attitude to racial prejudice amongst some police officers is not often apparent until it manifests itself outwardly in behaviour.

It must not be overlooked that a great number of police constables serving as patrol officers are young in age and young in service. In many cases, the young officer is still adjusting his attitudes and is vulnerable to all the ill-advised philosophies of his colleagues. This is the hidden element in an officer's formative years and while much can be done to insist that his personal philosophies and attitudes are subordinated to those of the service, formal training on race relations needs to be supplemented by a conscious effort on the part of all officers to ensure their conduct does not reflect discriminatory behaviour against ethnic groups. It requires a sustained effort by supervisors to ensure that racially prejudiced behaviour is identified and eliminated.

In the context of the Brixton disorders, racial prejudice was found to have alienated the police from the local community and the further criticism of harassment was levelled by the older and younger generations of black people. As Lord Scarman observed, 'The belief here is as important as the fact.'[6] What is undoubtedly true is that one incident of racially prejudiced behaviour can be exaggerated by repetition, fuelled by rumour and gathers credibility in the process. The beliefs can only be contradicted by facts but where the distinction between belief and fact becomes blurred, it is difficult to convince those who make allegations of racial prejudice or harassment that such allegations are groundless.

The merits or otherwise of the existing system of investigating complaints against the police are examined later[7] but there is little doubt that many members of the public have little confidence in the system despite the injection of an independent element into the procedures by the Police Act 1976. It was hardly surprising therefore that Lord Scarman heard much evidence during his enquiry to support the view that while the police continued to investigate complaints against other police officers, many people, particularly among the ethnic groups, had no faith in the impartiality and, by implication, the efficiency of the system.[8]

The greatest danger in losing the support of the public on account of an unsatisfactory system of investigating complaints is that many people will refrain from complaining at all and justified criticism of police action will be stifled. No believer in the democratic society should tolerate the stifling of criticism and Lord Scarman had no hesitation in concluding that the present system was unsatisfactory and ineffective. 'Unless and until there is a system for judging complaints against the police which commands the support of the public, there will be no way in which the atmosphere of distrust and suspicion between the police and the community in places like Brixton can be dispelled.'[9]

The third criticism levelled at the police as being a contributory factor to the disturbances was that of unimaginative and inflexible policing. The basis of this criticism was that the police in Brixton were alleged to be insensitive to local opinion, were unimaginative and uncomprehending in their dealings with the ethnic minorities. It was also said that the police had their priorities wrong and that a meaningful discussion of policing policies with local community leaders would have led to a more responsive and responsible attitude to local problems. This inevitably raises questions of local accountability in matters of policing which, in turn, conflict with the established principle of operational independence. The issue at Brixton was the allegation that the police merely paid lip-service to the notion of consultation with the community and, in reality, felt that there were operational matters related to the control of serious crime which were not the public's business.

It was not suggested that the rule of law was being questioned or that all members of the public, whether black or white, should not be dealt with equally. It was contended that since the police were vested with considerable discretion in enforcing the law, that the discretion should be exercised consistently. This was a further limb to the issue of harassment. It was argued that the police had adopted the practice of seeking out, pursuing and arresting criminals irrespective of the effect of these methods on innocent people.[10]

The regulation of police discretion has always proved a difficult area and one which has been sadly neglected as a necessary ingredient of training. The issue of discretion is discussed later[11] but the allegation of inflexibility by the police carried with it the suggestion that the professional judgement of senior officers was unsound. The failure to consult with community leaders when planning a special operation against street crime and burglary was highlighted by Lord Scarman as an example of the rigid attitude adopted by the police in Brixton which led to the breakdown in the relationship between the police and the community.[12]

From the police point of view, they thought it neither desirable nor necessary to consult community leaders before deciding to mount the operation against street crime. They felt that any

advance notice of the operation or consultation before the event
would jeopardise its success. Similarly, they regarded the suggested need for consultation as an unwarranted intrusion upon
their operational independence and professional judgement. Lord
Scarman considered that the police made an error of judgement
and said, 'The proposition that it interferes, or may undermine,
independence of judgement is a "non-sequitur"; for consultation
informs judgement; it does not pre-empt it.'[13]

Lord Scarman recognised that some police operations must
remain secret since it would be futile if criminals could anticipate
and frustrate police action but he added that there were some
operations which required the support and approval of the local
community if they were to be successful in the long term. He
thought that street operations belonged to this class for they were
dependent upon a stop and search procedure which was bound to
inconvenience, and might well embarrass and anger, innocent
people who were stopped.[14] He concluded that in areas such as
Brixton where the impact of such operations would be felt directly
by despairing and sensitive young black men, there was a clear
need for a local understanding of what the police intended to do.[15]

Such conclusions are reached with the benefit of hindsight. If
the police saturation operation had been successful in reducing
the level of street crime and no disturbances had occurred, the
community might well have regarded it as an unqualified success.
In the event, the outbreak of disorder and rioting, viewed *ex post
facto*, was attributed directly to 'hard policing' and the effects of
Operation 'Swamp'. Lord Scarman concluded that if there had
been local consultation with local community leaders beforehand
as to the wisdom of mounting the operation, he did not believe it
could have been authorised. He felt that if policing attitudes and
methods had been adjusted to deal fully with the problems of
policing a multi-racial society, there would have been a review in
depth of the public order implications of the operation, which
would have included local consultation.[16]

Doubt was also cast on the efficacy of a street saturation
operation. There was no clear evidence that such an operation
diminished street crime since it may well drive it elsewhere. After
the operation it returned and it was, therefore, only a short term
solution to the problem. The long term strategy should be to
develop a style of policing which was designed to secure public
approval.[17]

It must be said that these general criticisms may be valid but what happened at Brixton on that April weekend? The incident which sparked off the disturbances on the Friday evening was nothing to do with a saturation operation. A police officer had stopped a youth who was being pursued by two or three other black youths. It was found that the youth had a serious wound between his shoulder blades but the officer's attempt to explain he was not arresting the youth was futile. The officer was jostled by the black youths and the injured youth ran off. The latter sought and obtained assistance from a white family and a taxi was called. The youth was seen to get into the taxi by two other police officers who were aware of the earlier incident.

On stopping the taxi, the police officers found that the youth's wound was serious and attempted first aid while an ambulance was called. A group of 30–40 black youths arrived and assumed the officers were injuring the youth. The injured youth was carried off by the crowd and taken by car to hospital. That should have been the end of the incident but the officer's call for assistance had been answered by other officers who pursued the group of black youths. The youths responded by throwing bricks and bottles and disorder escalated. About an hour later, order had been restored but not before six police officers had been injured, four police vehicles damaged and six persons arrested.

The incident, by any standards, had been a serious one but where had the prejudice been – who had pre-judged what the officers were doing with the injured youth? Who was being harassed and by whom? The local police commander decided to consult the local community leaders and give them a true account of the incident in order to dispel rumours. They were invited to the police station, a decision referred to by Lord Scarman as 'good imaginative policing'.[18]

The consultations touched on the number of police deployed in the area and the community leaders advised a reduction. This was acted upon to the extent that patrols were reduced in the area of the local Youth and Community Centre. The need to continue with the saturation operation was not apparently discussed but it was decided to continue it. Lord Scarman understood why it was decided to continue with the operation since street crime was a grave matter in Brixton, upon which the silent law-abiding majority of residents felt very strongly.[19] Nevertheless, the events of the following day prompted Lord Scarman to say that the wise course would have been to have discontinued the operation.[20]

The disturbances on the Saturday arose from an incident during the late afternoon when two plain clothes officers decided to check the driver of a stationary car for suspected possession of drugs. The driver was initially co-operative but he objected to his vehicle being searched. The incident attracted a group of some 30 youths and when one of the youths obstructed one of the officers, he was arrested. The arrested youth was placed in a police van and, with difficulty, it was driven off. Bottles and missiles were thrown and more crowds gathered. They were in a hostile mood and a police van was overturned and set alight. The senior police officer present called for reinforcements and succeeded in dispersing the crowd of youths by a baton charge.[21]

This success was short-lived. Violence erupted again and unprotected police officers were subjected to a battery of missiles including bricks, bottles, pieces of broken metal railings and ultimately, petrol bombs. The arrival of protective shields brought little relief. Vehicles were being overturned and set on fire. The shields proved ineffective against the increasing use of petrol bombs. The petrol ran under the shields and set fire to the officers' clothing. Police casualties were mounting and withdrawal was the only course. The crowd, now transformed into a rioting mob, set fire to a local public house.

As the situation grew worse, an attempt was made at mediation between the police and the crowd. The mediators included two members of Lambeth Borough Council, responsible for the Brixton area, and their suggestion that the police withdraw was rejected by the senior police officer present. When the mediators approached the crowd, they were seized and the crowd spelled out their terms for dispersing – the withdrawal of the police, an end to harassment and the release of those arrested. The police commander doubted that the rioters would disperse even if they said they would and, in any event, he would have been reluctant or even unwilling to leave the streets at the mercy of the mob whatever the pressure. A further demand from the crowd was that they wanted to put their case to the media but the intervention of more missiles heralded the end of any meaningful attempt at negotiation and consultation.

As the disorder continued, the police were subjected to further attacks by petrol bombs and missiles and many persons seized the opportunity to embark on a systematic course of looting in areas away from the general disorders. There is little doubt that the police were under a concentrated attack by youths who were giving vent to their hostile feelings. The hostility of the crowd prevented the fire appliances from dealing with the numerous fires now raging in the area. Four appliances were abandoned and other appliances and ambulances responding to calls for assistance were attacked and the occupants injured.

The police with great courage and determination attempted to clear an area in which the fire appliances could operate but they sustained heavy casualties in doing so. The fire officers also responded bravely in the face of collapsing buildings, difficulty with hoses and the relentless hail of missiles. At one stage, the senior police officer present turned the hoses on the crowd to avoid his officers being overrun – unorthodox perhaps, but extremely effective. The crowd fell back and the firemen were able to continue. Further reinforcements enabled the police to consolidate their position and by the late evening the main disorders were over. The total of 279 policed officers injured is proof enough of the concerted and hostile attack on the forces of law and order who stared anarchy in the face.

Lord Scarman summarised the events of that day as follows:

> The police had undergone an experience, till then unparalleled on the mainland of the United Kingdom. Within the community there were some who saw disorder as an opportunity for publicised protest; but many more were saddened and uncertain at the implications of the events. It was clear to all, however, that the scars of what had happened would linger in Brixton, and particularly in the relationship between the police and public, for a long time to come.[22]

On the following day, further disorders occurred during the late afternoon which followed a similar pattern to those on the previous day. Brixton Police Station, itself, came under threat from a large crowd of black youths but these were dispersed by a group of mounted officers. The attacks on the police were less intense than the previous day but no less severe in their consequences. A further 122 police officers were injured and 61 police vehicles damaged or destroyed. It was apparent that many people from outside the area of Brixton were involved and it can be assumed that they were attracted by the media coverage of the events. It is also clear that young blacks, elated by their defiance of the police, were anxious to exploit the situation to the full.

Lord Scarman concluded that the disorders were communal disturbances arising from a complex political, social and economic situation which is not special to Brixton and that they were essentially an outburst of anger and resentment by young black people against the police.[23] If these two conclusions are analysed, it surely cannot mean that the young blacks blamed the police for the political, social and economic conditions. Where people resent the established society they cannot attack the abstract elements of society such as the constitution or the government. They can do so verbally, but violent protest can only be directed against the police, the visible and tangible symbol of authority.

Although the events at Brixton were stated to be unparalleled, this was due to the high number of police and civilian casualties and the extent of the damage to buildings and vehicles. A parallel situation had occurred in the St Paul's area of Bristol in April 1980 when a group of black youths resented a police raid on a local cafe where warrants had been executed under the Licensing Act and Misuse of Drugs Act. While officers were inside the cafe, a crowd gathered and became more hostile as the numbers increased. The police were then attacked with stones and other missiles and were under virtual siege in the cafe.

Assistance was sought from other areas of Bristol and a group of 20 officers succeeded in rescuing their colleagues in the cafe but not before a police vehicle had been overturned by a group of 12 black youths and set on fire. As the police withdrew from the scene, the situation appeared to have eased but violence flared again when a group of police officers came under severe attack from bricks, slates, concrete, bottles and other missiles. A group of 50–60 police officers were confronted by a large crowd including some 200 black youths. Although some shields had been issued to protect the officers the ferocity of the attack compelled the police to fall back.

The Chief Constable of the area, being present and only too aware of the casualties being sustained, faced a difficult decision. Of the 50–60 police officers present, 22 had been injured and a further 27 had minor injuries. In addition, 21 police vehicles had been severely damaged including six which had been burned and destroyed. The Chief Constable, realising his officers were overwhelmed, decided to withdraw in order to re-group and return with reinforcements. The object was to ensure a speedy return to law and order with a minimum of bloodshed and he felt that no useful purpose would be served by the remainder of the police officers staying in the immediate area. It was hoped that the removal of the police – the object of the violence – would quieten the crowd and help to restore order.

The Home Secretary, in addressing Parliament on the disturbances, commented that what had begun as a normal operation into possible criminal offences had turned sharply and unexpectedly into serious public disorder. Referring to the looting which had taken place during the enforced absence of the police, he said that the lawlessness which followed was inexcusable. He added that however quickly or fiercely public disorder occurred, the police must be able swiftly to restore the peace and enforce the law. The Home Secretary stressed that if the police wished to maintain order by traditional methods, police forces must be able to call rapidly on sufficient trained officers and he called for a thorough and urgent examination of the arrangements for handling spontaneous public disorder. He welcomed the proposed enquiry into racial disadvantage in the area and the decision of the local authorities concerned to examine how good community relations could be strengthened.

Several significant points arose from an analysis of the incident at Bristol which occurred some twelve months before Brixton. At Bristol, there was a suggestion that the root of the problem was the relationship between the police and the black community in St Paul's but there had been no breakdown in relationships between the police and the community leaders. The police conceded, with hindsight, that the timing of the raid and other aspects of the operation could have been more imaginative but there was nothing inflexible in executing a lawful warrant. Police experience at that stage pointed to a 'low key' operation against an illegal drinking establishment with the attendant drug problems, a familiar aspect of policing any urban area which includes a substantial West Indian element.

There was no suggestion of a sustained police operation against street crime with the recurring complaints of racial prejudice and harassment. This was simple law enforcement in a sensitive area where the police were acting under the authority of a warrant. Would the reaction of the crowd have been any different if the warrant had been under the Theft Act or Explosives Act? It is doubtful if it would have been. The presence of a group of police officers at the cafe clearly attracted the interest of the crowd and here we can detect a common element with Brixton, namely, the presence of a large or unusual number of police officers in a sensitive black area is assumed by the collective view of those present to be harassment irrespective of the reason.

The lessons learned from the Bristol incident were numerous. Concern was expressed that the withdrawal of the police for a period of some four hours had left the area of St Paul's at the mercy of the looters and arsonists and that the public living in that area had been left unprotected. It is easy to criticise with hindsight but the Chief Constable, who alone actually faced the situation, was in no doubt. The extent of the violence was such that, had he not withdrawn, serious injury or loss of life was inevitable. His judgement and decision cannot really be challenged despite the clamour of criticism which suggested that a 'no-go' area was created. If that means that a particular area was left at the mercy of the mob to the exclusion of the police, then Brixton fared little better. On the Saturday, at the height of the disorders, the rioters had the run of Railton Road and Mayall Road and looting continued unchecked in the shopping centre of Brixton for some three hours before the police had assembled sufficient forces to regain the initiative and quell the disorders.[24]

At Brixton, also, the police were under great pressure and in danger of being overwhelmed but there they clung on desperately until reinforcements arrived. The injuries sustained were considerable and, in the final analysis, the cost has to be weighed against the effect of their resistance. Was there some principle at stake? In the light of the criticism at Bristol, it seems clear the police were determined to 'hang on' at all costs and any suggestion of withdrawal was rejected. There must have been occasions during the disorder when the police had to give ground in the face of hostility and it must be conceded that in the tactics of public order operations some re-grouping will be necessary in some situations in order to contain the crowd.

At Bristol, therefore, when the police withdrew, it was clearly intended that they should re-group and together with reinforcements go back into the area of disorder and quell the riot. It was reasonable to assume that reinforcements were readily available and the delay of four hours, due to the organisational and logistical problems, was not foreseeable when the decision to withdraw was made. The problem, highlighted by the experience at Bristol, was how to provide a sufficient body of officers at short notice to deal with spontaneous public disorder. An urgent examination of the problems involved was made and forces reviewed their training, equipment and mutual aid arrangements.

Despite this exercise, the situation which developed at Brixton enabled the rioters to exploit the delay in the police response to the disorder. When the disorder is spontaneous, there is bound to be some delay and it may often be fortuitous whether there are sufficient resources immediately available to respond. In the initial stages, some casualties may be inevitable until reinforcements and protective equipment arrive. In that difficult first phase, it is going to be a brave man – or a fool – who is going to state categorically that he will never withdraw in any situation. Whether it is regarded as re-grouping or retreating will invariably depend on the interpretation each side puts on it.

Lord Scarman, in commenting on the Brixton disorders, pointed out that the disorders had revealed weaknesses in the capacity of the police to respond sufficiently firmly to violence in the streets.[25] In his proposals and recommendations on policing, he commented, 'Effective reinforcement arrangements both within and between police forces are particularly important, because the traditional British approach to handling disorder requires, if it is to be effective, the presence of large numbers of officers.'[26]

This, however, assumes that the traditional nature of public disorder remains unchanged. The sinister introduction of petrol bombs at Brixton was a new dimension for which the police were unprepared. The response by the Home Office was not merely to examine more effective means of protection against fire but to recommend that equipment such as water cannon, CS gas and plastic bullets should be available in reserve to police forces. The effectiveness of water in dispersing rioters was ably demonstrated at Brixton and gas proved equally effective at Toxteth (Liverpool) three months later.

The use of water hoses and canisters of gas were defended on the basis of necessity and there is little doubt that desperate measures were called for in each case, but there is nothing traditional in a police approach to public disorder where equipment is provided for offensive purposes. The obvious risk is an

escalation on either side with each trying to adjust to the
superiority of the other. The principle of the minimum use of force
would be difficult to sustain in such circumstances.

Another principle at stake is that of 'policing by consent' which
Lord Scarman emphasised in his report. 'If the police are to
secure the assent of the public for their actions they must strike an
acceptable balance between the three elements of their function.'[27] The three elements referred to by Lord Scarman are those
identified by Sir Richard Mayne when drawing up the instructions for the 'New Police of the Metropolis' in 1829, namely the
prevention of crime, the protection of life and property and the
preservation of public tranquillity.

Lord Scarman emphasises that the primary duty of the police is
to maintain the 'Queen's peace' and that a police officer's first
duty is to co-operate with others in maintaining 'the normal state
of society'. He considers the police officer's second duty is to
enforce the law but if law enforcement puts at risk public
tranquillity he will have to make a difficult decision.

> Inevitably there will be situations in which the public interest
> requires him to test the wisdom of law enforcement by its likely
> effect upon public order. Law enforcement, involving as it
> must, the possibility that force may have to be used, can cause
> acute friction and division in a community – particularly if the
> community is tense and the cause of the law-breaker not
> without support. 'Fiat justitia; ruat caelum'[28] may be apt for a
> judge; but it can lead a policeman into tactics disruptive of the
> very fabric of society.[29]

This statement of principle has been quoted in full since it is
crucial to the understanding of the police role in a democratic
society and it involves identifying operational priorities and
carefully weighing the likely effect of one upon the other. This is
the balance to which Lord Scarman refers and the conflict which
this can cause can only be solved by firstly giving priority to the
maintenance of public order and secondly by the constant and
commonsense exercise of police discretion.[30]

The subject of police discretion and how it is exercised 'lies at
the heart of the policing function' and the issue is fully discussed
later. It is sufficient at this stage to note the great importance that
Lord Scarman attaches to it since the good reputation of the police

as a force depends upon the skill and judgement which policemen display in performing their duties.[31] If the balance is achieved, therefore, it can only enhance the reputation of the police and this, in turn, will increase the support of the public on whose behalf the police act. Again, a brief glimpse of the wisdom of Sir Charles Rowan's statement of principle reveals the essence of policing by consent. 'The power of the police to fulfil their functions and duties is dependent upon public approval of their existence, actions and behaviour, and their ability to secure and maintain public respect.'

In the wake of Lord Scarman's report it was right that the police should conduct a careful self-examination. It has become customary to assess the effectiveness and efficiency of the police service by means of annual statistics, annual reports and other methods which have no real scientific basis but are merely indicators of performance. In the same way, it is difficult to assess public approval of the police system, its methods and conduct. The police complaints procedure is a limited method of indicating the worst excesses of police behaviour and the few genuine complaints tend to be submerged in a sea of trivial and vindictive matters which are an inevitable consequence of the lawful exercise of authority.

It is suggested that the events at Brixton and elsewhere were clear indications that the methods, indeed the existence, of the police in those areas, did not command public approval. How valid is that suggestion? Which sections of the public disapproved? The only way of accurately testing public opinion is by some form of referendum and even that may be a doubtful barometer. In a democracy, it is left to elected representatives at both national and local level to weigh public opinion and measure its effect. As far as Brixton is concerned, these elected representatives had been aware of hostility between the public and the police for some time long before the disorders.

In March 1979, the Lambeth Borough Council set up a formal enquiry into the nature of policing in Lambeth and its effect on the local community. The enquiry heard verbal and written evidence from a large cross section of the local community but the police refused to accept the invitation to give evidence since they doubted the true impartiality of the members of the enquiry. Since the enquiry was not conducted on a judicial basis, much of the evidence was not tested and this, together with the absence of any police comment, inevitably led to a published report which was highly critical of the local police and its methods. It described the police at Lambeth as an army of occupation and criticised the special patrol group (SPG) and its 'attacks' on the local people.

The report also criticised police raids on youth clubs, the attitude of the police towards the black community and it referred to abuses of interrogation procedures against juveniles. The working party concluded from the evidence presented to it that the treatment of juveniles in police stations presented a 'picture of violence, intimidation and induced confessions'. The accountability of the police through the complaints procedure was strongly criticised and the report, betraying its political flavour, suggested that the appointment of Community Relations Officers was a 'liberal facade for the increasingly centrally controlled militarisation of the police'.

The real issue was thrust into the open. The report was welcomed by the Lambeth Borough Council who endorsed the recommendations that the Metropolitan Police should be placed under the control of the Greater London Council. The local politicians were seeking control over the policing policies for the area. The SPG had been falsely projected as a sinister, ruthless group, heavily armed and highly trained to harass the citizens of Brixton and elsewhere. This propaganda campaign proved successful owing to the reluctance of the police to submit evidence to the working party in order to refute the allegations of police malpractice and oppressiveness.

The success of the propaganda campaign was also due to the high level of sensitivity in the area and the general belief, fuelled by rumour, that the police were conducting a conscious campaign of intimidation and harassment. The effect of the unchallenged statements forming the basis of the working party's report was summarised by Lord Scarman who had no doubt that the style, language and contents of the report succeeded only in worsening community relations with the police. He was also satisfied that it reflected attitudes, beliefs and feelings widely prevalent in Lambeth since 1979.[32]

The campaign by the Lambeth Borough Council to place the police under political control was part of a wider political movement, well recognised by the police themselves, to reform the independent status of the police and make them subordinate to the political wishes of local politicians. Historically, the fear of the public was that the police would become the arm of government yet here were indications of a desire that the police should become the arm of local government.

The legacy of Brixton and its disorders is a blurring of the two principles reiterated with such credibility by Lord Scarman. If policing by consent means that the police must operate in accordance with policies determined by local politicians so that the right balance is achieved, then the police can no longer enjoy that degree of independence which has been a feature of its development and effectiveness. At the core of the problem is accountability and this will be studied in some depth later.

If policing policies are sensitive to the needs of the community and the independence of the police, supported by police experience and profesional judgement, is seen to result in a balanced response to law enforcement, the clamour for greater accountability will cease. When a community feels that the independence of the police leads to unregulated and oppressive measures, concern for greater accountability is a natural consequence.

The dilemma identified at Brixton was how the police could cope with an increasing level of crime, particularly street robberies, by intensifying police activity when such activity antagonised a section of the community amongst which many of the criminals were to be found. The conclusion reached by Lord Scarman is that the police must strike a balance between the maintenance of order and the secondary function of law enforcement. The notion that this requires the police to 'go easy' when dealing with ethnic minorities in sensitive areas militates against the widely held belief that the police should enforce the law without fear or favour and should discharge their duties impartially.

In the Police evidence submitted to Lord Scarman, the apparent conflict was cogently expressed:

It is right that the integrity of the law should be preserved but the means to achieve this can be different. In short, therefore, it is patently obvious that when various social pressures and tensions exist within any particular community, it is imperative that police officers on duty in the area adopt a sensible and sensitive approach. This is not to say that they must negate their basic duty under the law or act otherwise than totally impartially, for it would surely be folly to expect the police to employ double standards of law enforcement to placate or stifle the protests of unreasonable activists or to show undue favour to racial minorities.[33]

There is little doubt that Brixton has written itself into the pages of police history and will be regarded as an important phase of police development. It will be seen as the time when the principles of policing were tested, evaluated and re-affirmed. As Lord Scarman, himself, said:

The relevance of Brixton was not that the principles of policing were wrong or that the law was incapable of coping. It was that the British public, including the British police, had not woken up to the problems in their inner cities and had not adjusted important old principles to a new and difficult and, to most people, unfamiliar situation.[34]

3 Police Ethics

The principles of policing which Lord Scarman identified in his Report[1] emphasised the need, widely recognised by police officers, to secure the trust, confidence, respect and support of the public. Only by insisting on high standards of professional conduct at all levels can these objectives be met since anything which falls short of the high standards expected by the public will lead to a lack of confidence, respect and support. A police service which alienates itself from the public it serves can hardly call itself a profession and cannot rely on the principle of policing by consent.

The historical survey in Chapter 1 touched on the influence of Colquhoun, Bentham and others during the period of reform. Their writings clearly influenced Peel and it is possible to trace the first signs of an ethical basis for an organised police force from their works. The utilitarian view advanced by Bentham[2] was essentially a philosophical and political doctrine which gave effect to the 'greatest good' principle. The law and its institutions were justified in restraining individual liberty in furtherance of this principle. Here was the rationale for an organised police system since restraint implied some means of coercion to ensure compliance. As Dicey commented, 'Nothing can be more necessary for the happiness of ordinary citizens than protection against robbery and physical violence.'[3]

Bentham recognised, however, that a system of police must be controlled since they would have far-reaching powers of interference. He advocated that the circumstances in which police action could be taken should be clearly defined by law and that the public should be informed that there could only be *legal* justification for interference with their security, their property and their honour. Powers would be controlled by limiting their exercise to particular occasions or for specific causes.

Bentham also accepted that although discretion was a necessary aspect of police power, any abuse of arbitrary power should be regulated by the principle that the more extreme measures should be sparingly used and that 'no method of prevention should be employed, which is likely to cause a greater mischief than the offence itself'.[4] He envisaged a general law of liberty and he considered that a free press, a representative Parliament, together with an independent and honest judiciary, would keep such a law alive in its purity and legality.[5]

The theme of liberty and justice as a basis for law, therefore, recognised that liberty was not unbounded but required some degree of restraint. It was also recognised that in regulating individual freedom it was necessary to ensure that the law and the means of enforcing it had to secure popular approval. There was an ethical basis for this view that the enforcement of the law had to satisfy certain criteria if it was to be an acceptable restraint on individual conduct.

One of the most important criteria was that any system of enforcement should be just or fair. Indeed, the very essence of justice is that it is concerned with the maintenance of a balance between individuals.[6] An extension of this view is that, prima facie, all human beings should be treated alike.[7] The concept of justice has also been connected with the 'common good'; that justice involves seeking the 'common good' by attending to the interests of all members of society with impartiality.[8]

Colquhoun had urged that any system of policing had to be well-regulated, energetic and conducted with 'purity, zeal and intelligence'[9] Peel had also recognised that in order to secure public approval and consent, his proposed new system of policing had to be characterised by a high standard of discipline and integrity. Integrity is associated with honesty and morality and great emphasis was placed on individual conduct. The wider aspects of police practice found an ethical basis in seeking to achieve a high standard of general conduct characterised by fairness, honesty and helpfulness.

The comparatively recent emergence of police ethics can be regarded as a reflection of professional maturity. A code of ethical conduct is usually associated with the long established professions such as medicine and law and the proposition that the police service is a profession implies that a recognised code of ethical conduct exists. The status of a profession also includes an element of trust, a degree of service and a high level of technical competence preceded by extensive training. A further feature is that a profession preserves its ethical code by a system of internal discipline and self-regulation.

An important characteristic of the police profession is the degree of trust imposed on the individual officer to discharge his duties faithfully according to law. The sworn declaration made by a recruit embodies an ethical statement of intent that he will serve the Queen in the office of constable without favour or affection, malice or ill-will and that he will, to the best of his skill and knowledge, discharge all duties faithfully according to law. This declaration identifies impartiality, fairness, benevolence and honesty as the basis for police conduct.

In some cases, the full impact of this declaration is soon lost amid the pressures of early training and operational duty and there is little scope to reinforce the importance of this declaration as a basis for an officer's duties. The officer is invariably subjected to a variety of internal and external influences which affect the manner in which he discharges his duties. To discharge his duties faithfully in all situations requires him to act in accordance not only with his legal powers but with a recognised pattern of conduct.

This pattern of conduct is regulated and influenced by internal instructions, local policy and the example of others but many decisions require the application of personal values. As individuals, our personal values may differ considerably since they have been moulded by a variety of factors. Obvious influences include family background, education and religion and these combine to provide a basis for private morality. Difficulties can arise where this private morality conflicts with professional standards of conduct – the high standards expected by the public and hopefully reflected in all departments of the police service.

Any discussion on ethical conduct among police officers may often provoke scepticism since an ethical code of conduct represents an ideal to which police officers should aspire. The sceptic finds it hard to accept that people can measure up to the ideal and he will often criticise or question the motives of the person concerned. Any attempt to suggest that there should be a higher code of conduct by which police conduct should be judged is often regarded as a further attempt to frustrate the police officer in the discharge of his duties.

At the other extreme is the idealist, himself, who is also a perfectionist and finds it difficult to accept anything less than the ideal. He contributes very little except to his own frustration. It is the realist who can make the greatest contribution because he recognises that although police conduct should be measured against a higher norm, he knows that there are practical and human limitations in achieving objectives. He recognises that different situations require different responses and that it is often difficult to translate general ethical principles into a ready solution in individual cases.

To the young and inexperienced officer there is often a conflict between his early training with its emphasis on a service ideal and his developing experience at street level. Being surrounded by more experienced officers, there is often pressure to imitate their conduct and become part of the group. The ideals of the service are soon lost amid the realities of police experience. The officer is often caught up in situations over which he feels he has little control and there is the risk that he will accept without question the action of colleagues which should be criticised. It is essentially a test of character when conflict arises between his loyalty to the service and his loyalty to his colleagues.

There is much to be gained by noting the approach to police ethics in the United States. Police systems in the United States, as in England, were formed in response to a common threat to the social order and established morality. The tradition of violence was transferred from the frontier to the developing urban areas and, in contrast to Peel's cautious restraint on police powers, reliance was placed on the tough armed police officer to control disorder and crime. The variety of police systems which emerged, being under local control, lacked the control, stability and reforming influence of a central authority.

Local police forces were kept under popular control by the appointment of chief officers who were responsible to local elected bodies. This often provided a climate in which local politicians perverted the course of justice and used the police for their own corrupt purposes. There was little supervision imposed on police practice and few guidelines on the exercise of their powers except those imposed by judicial review. The latter was principally concerned with admissions, confessions and the circumstances surrounding interrogation.

In England, the government was able to influence development by means of an inspectorate which examined efficiency and applied common standards and practices by way of administrative advice and directions. The police systems in the United States, with no such centralised supervision, witnessed the development of wide variations in police practice. In some areas, corruption was widespread and local courts would often tolerate illegal or irregular police conduct since public opinion invariably supported arbitrary police action, especially against unpopular minorities.

It is against this background that attempts were made to reform police systems in the United States in the early part of this century. One advocate for reform was August Vollmer, who held office as the chief of police in Berkeley, California, from 1909 to 1932. To him, the professional police officer was synonymous with a high standard of personal conduct. He should display physical and moral courage and have the capacity for compassion and the humane treatment of others. He encouraged educated police officers who would have a wider training in science, sociology and psychology – officers of 'all-round' ability who would represent a model of honesty and self-discipline and who would be regarded as incorruptible.

Vollmer considered that the police systems of the United States had failed the people they represented and he advocated the centralisation of local police forces into a single State Police which would be free from unscrupulous politicians and would consist of police officers of superior education, intelligence and character. His attempt to establish a centralised police system was frustrated by local resistance to any dispersal of control over the police. This resistance to change the basis of local police control has been a recurring feature of police history in both England and America.

There was also resistance to Vollmer's other attempts at reform but there is little doubt that his reforming influence and his emphasis on better education and a higher standard of professional integrity are still reflected in the modern police systems of the United States. It could be said that the nature of policing in America at that time provided a climate for reform and that the strong theme of professionalism, particularly in police departments on the western seaboard, stems from Vollmer's efforts to identify a police ethic.

Other advocates of reform such as Bruce Smith[10] also condemned improper police practices. Smith, a recognised authority on police administration, carried out numerous surveys to determine the extent of police misconduct. He was highly critical of the failure of police departments which failed to take proper steps to regulate illegal and improper practices and commented:

> Police interrogation under circumstances that infringe basic liberties guaranteed by the Constitution also raise disturbing questions as to the extent to which justice under law is accepted as a guide to conduct. Hence, until more responsible attitudes are assumed by portions of the rank and file, as well as by their police superiors, there can be no police profession in any worthwhile connotation of the term.[11]

The essential difference in the development of police systems in England and the United States lies in the degree of local control. Although both systems had their origins in the common law, they followed different paths. In the United States, the strong influence of local control made the police servants of policy whereas the more refined system of policing in England made them servants of the law. The structure of policing in England with its blend of local control and central supervision facilitated reforms which were designed to provide common practices and common standards of conduct.

Moreover, the English model, being independent of local political control, demonstrated its capacity to control police conduct by self-regulation. Common standards were secured by a statutory discipline code which covered a wide area of police impropriety which was regarded as unacceptable and inconsistent with any ethical code of conduct. Offences against the code included falsehood and prevarication, corrupt practice and the unlawful and unnecessary exercise of authority. This discipline code is still relied on as an effective internal measure for regulating improper police conduct.

There are, of course, other ways of regulating police conduct. In extreme cases, where an officer offends against the criminal law, he is amenable to the law as any other individual and cannot hide behind the discipline code. Similarly, an officer may also offend against the civil law and be held liable for actions in trespass, negligence, false imprisonment and other torts. By the Police Act 1964, a chief officer of police is now liable in respect of torts committed by constables under his direction and control.[12] This vicarious liability is similar to that of a master who is liable for the wrongful acts of his servant.

In determining whether police conduct has infringed the basic freedoms of the individual, reference is often made to constitutional law and, again, there is an interesting and useful comparison to be made between the British Constitution and that of the United States. It is often said that the British Constitution is unwritten yet the basis of freedom under the law can be traced back to Magna Carta in 1215. Article 39 sets out a famous declaration on equality under the law and the right of every free man to justice. King John had ignored the customary rights under common law and considered he could dispense justice as a personal favour. He was forced to concede to the demands of the barons and the Magna Carta has been interpreted throughout English history as a guarantee of civil liberties.

Article 39 can be freely translated, 'No free man shall be taken or imprisoned or disseised (deprived of his lands) or outlawed or in any way destroyed, nor will we go upon him nor put upon him, except by the lawful judgement of his peers or the law of the land.'[13] It was subsequently re-affirmed by successive monarchs and re-stated in the Petition of Right in 1628. This document, presented to Charles I by the English Parliament, contained a number of constitutional demands which were accepted. It reaffirmed the principle of *habeas corpus*[14] and declared arbitrary imprisonment as illegal.

A writ or order of *habeas corpus* is issued by a judge and requires a detained person to be brought before a court in order that the legality of the detention can be determined. In both England and the United States it remains as the chief safeguard against unlawful detention. This is not surprising since the legal systems of both countries are based on the common law. Insofar as police powers *vis à vis* the ordinary citizen is concerned, the absence of a written constitution in Britain means that there is no fundamental code of basic freedoms and rights to which the ordinary citizen can refer.

Dicey, a recognised authority on the British Constitution, related the fundamental rights of the individual to the concept of the rule of law. In echoes of Magna Carta, he stated that no man is punishable or can be lawfully made to suffer in body or goods except for a distinct breach of the law established in the ordinary legal manner before the ordinary courts of the land. Every man, whatever his rank or condition, is subject to the ordinary law of the land and amenable to the ordinary jurisdiction of the courts.

He added that the general principles of the Constitution were the result of judicial decisions determining the rights of private persons in particular cases brought before the courts, whereas under many foreign constitutions the security given to the rights of individuals results . . . from the general principles of the constitution.[15]

He went on to describe the British Constitution as a 'judge-made constitution' and the result of the ordinary law of the land. In this way the exercise of police powers was not arbitrary or absolute but discretionary and qualified and effective remedies existed to secure a person's release (writ of habeas corpus) and to obtain compensation for any unlawful act.

The American Constitution is discussed later and there are conflicting views as to the benefits of a written constitution. It is felt that grand principles of freedom, expressed in vague terms, still have to be related to individual cases. Nevertheless, there is little doubt that Americans cherish the freedoms enshrined in their Constitution and they are regarded as so fundamental that special procedures are required to amend them. This sets them above ordinary law; indeed, the Supreme Court can intervene if ordinary laws are inconsistent with the constitution. There is little doubt that public opinion is more easily mobilised in the defence of constitutional rights and this is important when police action is being judged.

In English law, the safeguards for the individual are invariably defined by case law. Many powers of arrest given by statute may be unlawful if certain conditions are not followed. The leading case on this issue is *Christie* v. *Leachinsky*.[16] The House of Lords set out certain principles concerning arrest, the essential one being that the person arrested must be informed of the true grounds for arrest. If not so informed but nevertheless seized, the police officer is liable for false imprisonment. The court stressed that technical or precise language was unnecessary and that the requirement did not exist if the accused knew from the circumstances why he was being detained or if the arrested person made it practically impossible for him to be informed.

Viscount Simon said, 'The matter is a matter of substance, and turns on the elementary proposition that in this country a person is, prima facie, entitled to his freedom and is only required to submit to restraints on his freedom if he knows in substance the reason why it is claimed that this restraint should be imposed.' He went on to emphasise that these conditions were not intended to constitute a formal or complete code but to indicate the general principles of the law on a matter of great importance.

This illustrates the difficulties in trying to establish a code of individual rights and it must be remembered that it is as important for the police officer to know the limits of his powers as it is for the ordinary citizen. Vagueness induces uncertainty and it is difficult to talk about the public consenting to be policed if the way in which the public expect to be policed or accept restraint on their freedom is imprecise.

These difficulties are perhaps best illustrated by two examples of case law relating to the right of the police to question people. In 1966, it was ruled that a person was not guilty of obstructing a police officer in the execution of his duty if he refused to tell the officer his name and address or where he was going. A citizen was under no legal obligation to answer questions by the police.[17] In a later case, a police officer was assaulted by a person who did not wish to speak to him. The officer had touched him on the shoulder and had been struck in the face. The court held that the person was guilty of assaulting the officer in the execution of his duty.[18]

This decision has been criticised since it tended to confuse the nature of the officer's duty. If the police officer had no right to detain a person for questioning, even momentarily, then that person was under no duty to answer questions or to remain. In practice, the public accept a moral duty to assist the police but there will always be the unco-operative person to test the limits of police powers and patience. It is then that legal duties have to be determined so that the police can act without infringing the rights of the individual.

These constitutional safeguards are supplemented not only by statutory limitations but also by national and local administrative directions and guidance. The Judges' Rules, for example, first formulated by the judges of the Kings Bench Division of the High Court in 1912, and subsequently revised, set out firm guidelines regarding the questioning of suspects which, if ignored, could result in any admission or confession being rendered inadmissible as evidence.

The rules are based on several principles but the overriding principle is that any statement, either verbal or written, made by an accused person to the police, must be made voluntarily in the sense that it has not been obtained from him by fear of prejudice or hope of advantage, exercised or held out by a person in authority or by oppression. In support of this' principle, the rules provide that a person should be cautioned at a particular stage in the questioning process so that an accused can exercise his privilege against self-incrimination and remain silent.

The rules are supplemented by administrative directions which provide for a record of the interrogation to be kept and the rights of the accused to speak with a solicitor or a friend to be considered. The comfort and refreshment of persons being questioned is a further consideration and an accused person is entitled to a written statement of any charges being made against him. The whole emphasis is that a person subjected to police questioning should be humanely and properly treated and the procedures also ensure that evidence obtained by way of a written or verbal statement can properly be admitted in evidence.

The questioning of persons in police custody is a 'low visibility' area of police activity which is often the subject of criticism, inside and outside the court, and one example of impropriety or oppressive conduct is sufficient to provoke a clamour for reform. The Judges' Rules have no legal force and failure to observe them does not necessarily result in an admission or confession being excluded from evidence. The Royal Commission on Criminal Procedure recommended that the rules should be replaced by a statutory code of practice.

The basis for this recommendation was the Commission's view that the Rules had been and still were the subject of persistent controversy. This was because of their uncertain status and that initially they had represented a first conscious effort within the pre-trial procedure to set out a considered balance between the need to protect the rights of the individual suspect and the need to give the police sufficient powers to carry out their task. In seeking this balance they acknowledged that any rules which specified a citizen's rights must also impose duties on society generally and on those who had to question him.[19]

The treatment of suspects in custody was only one area of police activity which was closely examined by the Royal Commission. The Royal Commission, in embarking on a comprehensive review of the whole criminal process, recognised increasing public anxiety about the rising level of crime and its relationship with the police role in investigation and the subsequent prosecution of offenders.

On one side, it was asserted that the job of the police in fighting crime and of ensuring that offenders, and particularly dangerous professional criminals, were brought to justice was being made unwarrantably difficult by the restraints of criminal procedure; and on the other side that the use of their powers of investigation by the police was often open to grave question.[20]

The Report refers to the Commission's terms of reference and the concept of a fundamental balance between the interest of the whole community and the rights and liberties of the individual citizen.[21] It is clear that ethical considerations were not ignored.

What are the rights and liberties of the individual which are assumed to provide part of the balance? Who gives them and what justifies them? Are they all of equal weight; all equally and totally negotiable or are some natural, absolute, fundamental, above the law, part of the human being's birthright?[22]

If the rights and liberties of the individual are a fundamental aspect of police conduct, then there must be some ethical code, some higher norm against which such conduct can be measured. In the majority of countries throughout the world, these rights and liberties can be found in the constitution and historically, the American Constitution has no equal as a written statement of ethical principles designed for the protection of the individual.

The Founding Fathers of the American Constitution took notice of Thomas Jefferson's firm advice to incorporate a written Bill of Rights. Consequently, ten amendments were added which established a Bill of Rights. For the purposes of controlling police conduct, the following three amendments are still valid and the subject of decisions by the Supreme Court.

'IV – The right of the people to be secure in their persons, houses, papers and effects, against unreasonable searches and seizures, shall not be violated, and no warrants shall issue, but upon probable cause, supported by oath or affirmation, and particularly describing the place to be searched, and the persons or things to be seized.

V – No person shall answer for a capital, or otherwise
infamous crime, unless on a presentment or indictment of
a Grand Jury . . . nor shall any person be subject for the
same offence to be twice put in jeopardy of life or limb;
nor shall be compelled in any criminal case to be witness
against himself, nor be deprived of life, limb or property,
without due process of law; nor shall private property be
taken for public use without just compensation.

VI – In all criminal prosecutions, the accused shall enjoy the
right to a speedy and public trial, by an impartial jury of
the State and district wherein the crime shall have been
committed . . . and to be informed of the nature and cause
of the accusation; to be confronted with the witnesses
against him; to have compulsory process for obtaining
witnesses in his favour, and to have the assistance of
counsel for his defence.

The effect of these amendments on current police practice in the
United States is perhaps best illustrated by the landmark case on
a suspect's rights, *Miranda* v. *Arizona* (1966).[23] The familiar
'Miranda Warnings' are a reminder to a person in custody of his
constitutional rights and 'You have the right to remain silent and
refuse to answer questions' is almost as familiar as the English
counterpart of 'You are not obliged to say anything unless you
wish to do so.' One variation in the American practice is that the
suspect is asked 'Do you understand?' after each part of the
warning.

The suspect is further warned that anything he says may be
used against him; that he has the right to consult an attorney
before speaking to the police and to have an attorney present
during any questioning. He is advised that if he cannot afford an
attorney, one will be provided without cost and he is reminded
that his right to remain silent remains until he has had an
opportunity of consulting with one.

An individual may waive his right to have an attorney present
or his right to remain silent provided it can be shown that the
waiver was voluntary, knowingly done and intelligently done.
The prosecution have the onus of proving the waiver and the
courts tend to adopt a rigid practice of excluding any evidence

obtained without the warnings being given. The court will take into account certain factors in determining whether a defendant's rights were voluntarily, knowingly and intelligently waived. These would include the fact that the person was under the influence of drugs or drink; whether a language barrier exists; whether the individual has a low IQ or where it is obvious to the police officer that the defendant is not 'too bright'. Further considerations would be the age of the defendant, whether he had had previous contact with the police and whether the questioning was of a coercive nature.

The Miranda case also emphasised the wider disadvantages to the prosecution if the warnings were not strictly followed. Derivative evidence, often referred to as 'the fruit of the poisonous tree' doctrine, would also be excluded so that evidence obtained by virtue of an inadmissible confession, such as the recovery of stolen goods hidden by the accused, would also be rendered inadmissible.

The English courts adopt a different view which may reflect the relative extent of police misconduct and the measures necessary to secure compliance with established procedures designed to safeguard the rights of the accused person. Wigmore, a noted authority on evidence, held the view that the judicial rules of evidence were never intended to be an indirect process of punishment against the police and to exclude evidence as a penal measure for police malpractice was against the interests of the public. He considered that if a police officer obtains a confession by some improper or underhand method, the remedy is to punish the officer and not to exclude the confession since facts discovered in consequence of an inadmissible confession might have verified it.

An early English case[24] on the subject involved a woman who had confessed to knowledge of stolen property but the court found that the confession had been obtained by promises of favour and it was excluded. The fact that stolen property was found concealed in her bed, however, was admitted and the court said, 'this principle respecting confessions has no application whatsoever as to the admission or rejection of facts, whether the knowledge of them be obtained in consequence of an extorted confession or whether it arises from any other source'. A more recent judicial comment was given by Lord Diplock in 1979[25] when he stated:

It is no part of a judge's function to exercise disciplinary powers over the police or prosecution as respects the way in which evidence to be used at the trial is obtained by them. If it was obtained illegally there will be a remedy in civil law; if it was obtained legally but in breach of the rules of conduct for the police, this is a matter for the appropriate disciplinary authority to deal with.[26]

The obvious value in admitting this evidence of subsequent facts is that it established the *truth* of the original confession, no matter how it was obtained, but the admissibility of the evidence was still restricted by the court's comment that 'facts thus obtained must be fully and satisfactorily proved without calling in the aid of any part of the confession from which they have been derived'. The American approach is exemplified by Oliver Wendell Holmes[27] in his statement that 'It is a lesser evil that some criminals should escape than that the government should have played an ignoble part.'

The Report of the Royal Commission on Criminal Procedure referred to the automatic exclusion rule which operates in America and took the view that its use appeared justified as a deterrent to unlawful conduct by the police and to preserve the integrity of the court by preventing its involvement in illegal activity.[28] The Report comments that the United States Supreme Court had felt constrained to develop the rule to protect the citizen's constitutional rights and that the Supreme Court's assumption of this role derived its moral and political force from its responsibility to protect and interpret the rights of the citizens of the United States that are enshrined in the Bill of Rights.

Furthermore, doubts are raised as to whether an automatic exclusionary rule that seeks to deter improper conduct actually achieves that objective. The Report refers to the comments of Chief Justice Burger:

> Some of the most recent cases in the Supreme Court reveal, almost plaintively, an unspoken hope that if judges say often and firmly that deterrence is the purpose, police will finally notice and be deterred. I suggest that the notion was never more than wishful thinking on the part of the courts. . . . We can well ponder whether any community is entitled to call itself an 'organised society' if it can find no way to solve the problem except by suppression of truth in search of truth.[29]

The Report, in dealing with this fundamental issue of police conduct, maintained that English judges had not seen themselves as having that function of controlling improper police behaviour. They had never subscribed to exclusion of evidence under a 'disciplinary principle' and they had favoured the application of a 'reliability principle'.[30]

The Royal Commission also identified a third principle concerning the conduct of criminal investigations and this is referred to as the 'protective principle'.[31] The rationale for this principle is found in the Commission's view that where certain standards are set for the conduct of criminal investigations, the public have a right to expect that they will be treated in accordance with such standards. If they were not treated properly, they should not be exposed to risk and the investigator should not gain any advantage. If the principle was applied, the exclusion of irregularly obtained evidence was the price to be paid for securing public confidence in the rules of criminal procedure and the fairness of the system.[32]

The issue of police conduct in relation to the questioning of suspects and persons in custody is very important since it is central to the whole system of criminal justice and ultimately affects the way in which public confidence in the police is shaped. There is obvious merit in the view of the Royal Commission that Parliament should draw up a code of conduct for the police on a statutory basis and not leave it to the court's discretion to regulate improper practice.

The Royal Commission also examined the whole process of police investigation into crime and concluded that at every stage there has to be a balance between the extent and effect of the investigative powers and the rights of the individual. The Commission also concluded that the availability of coercive powers in the investigative process requires general justification and the exercise of these powers in a particular case should be warranted by the specific circumstances and be capable of immediate challenge and subsequent review.

One of the greatest difficulties noted by the Royal Commission was the complexity of the law under which the police operated and they referred to a lack of clarity and an uneasy and confused mixture of common law and statutory powers of arrest.[33] Apart from the difficulties presented to the police the Commission rightly pointed out that it is scarcely surprising if the citizen is uncertain of his rights.[34] This, of course, stems from the nature of the British Constitution which has never been codified and the vagueness surrounding the variety of common law powers which have evolved over several centuries.

In order to remedy this unsatisfactory situation, the Commission recommended that the existing provisions should be reformulated and restated in modern terms. They recognised that the police must have certain investigative powers but that the exercise of these powers and the controls upon them must command public confidence. In evaluating the existing procedures and in making proposals for change, fairness, openness and workability were the principles to be applied.[35]

The general conclusions in the Report were clearly an attempt to provide a consistent framework, based on openness and fairness, which recognised the practical necessity for police powers in investigation of crime but also acknowledged the rights of the individual with whom the police may come into contact.

Consequently, it was recommended that coercive powers should be placed upon a single statutory footing;[36] powers to stop and search persons and vehicles should be rationalised;[37] warrants to enter and search premises should not give rise to general searches;[38] the use of arrest should be restricted to cases where it is necessary to achieve specific purposes – the application of a 'necessity principle';[39] existing powers of arrest without warrant should be placed on a consistent footing;[40] detention following arrest should be restricted in accordance with the 'necessity principle';[41] the common law power to search a person on arrest should be placed on a statutory footing.[42]

The rationale behind these measures for reform clearly has an ethical basis and they are characterised by a common thread of fairness to the individual without frustrating the role of the police in the investigation of crime. If existing police practice can aspire to an ethical ideal, then there should be no concern or sensitivity over proposals which advocate more openness. To adopt a defensive and protective stance towards existing police practice merely gives support to those who believe that oppressive and unjust practices do exist. The stifling of criticism is the first tactic of a totalitarian regime and it was the very nature of such a regime which first gave rise to the notion of a police ethic.

The emergence of ethics as one measure of police profesionalism has been due to a number of factors allied to greater freedom, greater awareness of human and civil rights and to the advent of terrorism. The early impetus for a professional police ethic stemmed from the legacy of the Second World War and in the iniquitous laws promulgated by the Third Reich which were ruthlessly enforced by the Geheime Staatspolizei (Gestapo). A ruthless policy of investigation, torture and extermination left its indelible mark on the conscience of Europe and provoked a movement to establish a code of ethics for the police which would have universal approval.

The United Nations Universal Declaration of Human Rights in 1948 was the starting point but it was not surprising that the European nations, which had suffered enemy occupation and the effect of arbitrary power, recognised the need to identify and safeguard fundamental human rights. These rights were basically a codification of those values already established in the constitutions of western democracies and were set out in the European Convention for the Protection of Human Rights and Fundamental Freedoms. Although acknowledging the United Nations Universal Declaration of Human Rights, it sought to restrict its application to those countries which had a common heritage of political traditions, ideals, freedom and the rule of law.

In 1979, the Council of Europe issued a Declaration on the Police[43] which was based on the premise that the full exercise of human rights and fundamental freedoms, guaranteed by the European Convention on Human Rights and other national and international instruments, had as a necessary basis the existence of a peaceful society and that the police played a vital role in maintaining law and order. It was stated that the police were frequently called upon to intervene in conditions which are dangerous for their members, and that their duties were made yet more difficult by rules of conduct which were not sufficiently and precisely defined. It was felt that the protection of human rights would be improved if there were generally accepted rules concerning the professional ethics of the police which took into account the principles of human rights and fundamental freedoms.

The code of ethics set out in the Declaration on the Police contains sixteen articles. They require, *inter alia*, that a police officer shall fulfil his legal duty to protect his fellow citizens and the community against violent, predatory and other harmful acts as defined by law.[44] He should act with integrity, impartiality and dignity and refrain from and vigorously oppose all forms of corruption.[45] Summary executions, torture and other forms of inhuman or degrading treatment or punishment remain prohibited in all circumstances and a police officer should disobey orders involving such measures.[46] A police officer should obey lawful orders and oppose violations of the law but no criminal or disciplinary action should be taken against a police officer who refuses to carry out an unlawful order.[47]

In addition, a police officer should not co-operate in the tracing, arresting, guarding or conveying of persons who are not suspected of illegal acts, but are searched for, detained or prosecuted because of their race, religion or political belief.[48] In carrying out his duties, a police officer should act with determination but should never use more force than is necessary.[49] Clear and precise instructions should be given to police officers as to the manner and circumstances in which they should use arms.[50] A police officer should obtain medical aid for any person in his custody and take measures to preserve his life and health.[51] He should keep secret all confidential matters coming to his notice except where his duties or the law require otherwise.[52]

Several of these articles may appear rather remote from a police officer's duties in modern society but it is important that the historical events which prompted the Universal Declaration of Human Rights are not forgotten. They have direct relevance to the principle of policing by consent since the last article states that a police officer who complies with the provisions of this Declaration is entitled to the active moral and physical support of the community he serves.[53]

It is interesting to note that there is some suggestion here of a contract between the police and the community – a *quid pro quo* that if the police conduct themselves in accordance with a set of values identified and accepted by all as equitable and just, then the community will actively support the police function in preserving law and order in society. A further benefit which arises from an established code of police ethics is that it establishes principles against which police practices and policies can be measured.

It is not sufficient that an ethical code of conduct should be an abstract notion which has universal approval without universal application. It should permeate into every aspect of the police function; individual officers should make a conscious effort to regulate the wide discretionary aspect of their duties so that the discretion is regarded not as absolute, but qualified by a pattern of ideals and values acceptable to society.

This poses the questions as to where an individual officer may look for guidance and how he can judge the morality of his actions. It is recognised that his legal powers and internal regulations will be a strong controlling influence but there remains a wide area of personal conduct which relies on strength of character, self-discipline and personal values. It is significant that the emergence of police ethics has been more marked in the United States and this may well be due to the large number and variety of law enforcement agencies which exist and the lack of any central supervision or common standards.

It was noted that the American courts adopted a more rigid exclusion rule with regard to evidence which had been improperly obtained in an effort to deter improper conduct and the reputation for corruption in some areas provoked an increasing desire for greater professionalism among police officers. In the early stages, reforming influences such as August Vollmer attempted to increase police professionalism by applying scientific techniques and by increasing educational standards. While this certainly improved the public image of the police it did little to influence widespread corruption and malpractice.

The ideals expressed by Vollmer and others included a requirement for absolute integrity as a measure of professionalism but while many accepted this as a worthy aim they gave very little practical effect to these ideals. In the period immediately after the Second World War, there appeared to be a more widespread concern about police professionalism with more emphasis on the conduct of individual officers. This was in support of the wider ideals expressed in the United Nations Universal Declaration of Human Rights and complemented it insofar that a code of police ethics, faithfully observed, would preserve the basic rights of individuals who came into contact with the police.

This was followed by a code of ethics drawn up by the International Association of Chiefs of Police which again emphasised personal conduct and responsibilities. It is repeated here to illustrate the strong appeal to the individual officer to recognise the moral and ethical basis of his profession.

LAW ENFORCEMENT CODE OF ETHICS

AS A LAW ENFORCEMENT OFFICER, my fundamental duty is to serve mankind; to safeguard lives and property; to protect the innocent against deception, the weak against oppression or intimidation, and the peaceful against violence or disorder; and to respect the constitutional rights of all men to liberty, equality, and justice.

I WILL keep my private life unsullied as an example to all; maintain courageous calm in the face of danger, scorn, or ridicule; develop self-restraint; and be constantly mindful of the welfare of others. Honest in thought and deed in both my personal and official life, I will be exemplary in obeying the laws of the land and the regulations of my department. Whatever I see or hear of a confidential nature or that is confided to me in my official capacity will be kept ever secret unless revelation is necessary in the performance of my duty.

I WILL never act officiously or permit personal feelings, prejudices, animosities, or friendships to influence my decisions. With no compromise for crime and with relentless prosecution of criminals, I will enforce the law courteously and appropriately without fear or favor, malice or ill will, never employing unnecessary force or violence and never accepting gratuities.

I RECOGNIZE the badge of my office as a symbol of public faith, and I accept it as a public trust to be held as long as I am true to the ethics of the police service. I will constantly strive to achieve these objectives and ideals, dedicating myself before God to my chosen profession . . . law enforcement.

Attempts were also made to provide a code of police ethics by the United Nations which would have universal appeal and encourage standardisation of police conduct in member countries. Emphasis was again placed on honesty, integrity, courtesy, self-control, compassion and tolerance and the code referred to the traditional role of helpfulness beyond the call of duty as a feature of police professionalism.

The emergence of police ethics in this country can be related to the codification of a number of fundamental statements of principle concerning police conduct and the importance to be attached to the rights of the individual citizen. Police practice has always been regulated by the constraints of law, regulations, directives and policy considerations all of which have some moral basis or reasoned source based on ethical grounds. They indicate the manner in which the police *ought* to carry out their duties. The difference between what *ought* to be done and what actually *is* done may be marginal but a code of ethics can indicate what *ought* to have been done when police conduct is under review. It can often provide the moral basis for police action to satisfy the test of justification.

To some police officers, the ideals expressed in a code of ethics do not correspond with the realities of police duty and have no immediate value or relevance to the practising police officer. Any code of ethics also suffers from being viewed as a 'holier than thou' philosophy which tends to frustrate any attempt to develop ethics as an essential element of police training. Yet it is significant that a simple research exercise carried out among police officers indicated that most officers had a higher opinion of their own ethical standards of conduct than they did of their colleagues.[54]

The individual officer has a great responsibility to do the right thing at the right time but difficulties arise in the interpretation of what is 'right' and it is here that ethical considerations come into play. The use of judgement and the exercise of discretion are so crucial to the effectiveness of the police role that it cannot be left to individual interpretation. A code of police ethics sets out the framework, the 'ground rules' for regulating individual action. The principle embodied in police ethics is that the role of the police should be so regulated by the application of internal ethical considerations that it becomes increasingly recognised by the public as being for the common good and a guarantee of individual freedom.

It has also been pointed out that a code of ethics might well protect the individual police officer who acted in good faith but erred in his judgement. By assessing his actions on ethical grounds, it could be more easily justified, even though wrong. Many actions suffer from the problem of being assessed as 'wrong' even though the initial decision was thought to be 'right'. Hindsight and post-incident criticism have often inhibited police action and led to informal and unregulated action. Alternatively, it has led to a defensive attitude when actions are questioned and a resentment that proper public concern is unwarranted.

It has also been suggested that a professional ethic would enhance the reputation of the service since the qualities of loyalty and integrity would reduce action based on self-interest and lead to a wider consideration of the interests of others. This should also influence those officers who, in the absence of any code of ethics, act in a manner which is against the public interest. That is, they adopt methods which, although designed to achieve proper objectives, are in themselves improper. There is no scope in a professional service for a philosophy whereby the 'end justifies the means'. At its worst it has all the hallmarks of a style of policing where authority is derived, not from the common consent of the people, but from an undemocratic regime which relies solely on the authority of the law itself.

It should not be overlooked that many police officers do adopt a proper professional approach to their duties. The countless examples of officers acting under a moral duty emphasise their genuine concern to serve and help the public. Many officers would recognise that their own values, standards and principles are reflected in the way they perform their duties and any suggestion that any of them would act in a way which is contrary to the ethical principles described would meet with immediate resentment. The majority of police officers are concerned about their standards of performance and are anxious to carry out their duties professionally and efficiently in the public interest.

What should be emphasised is that the professional relationship between the individual officer and the public is one of trust. The public rely on the individual police officer to use his considerable powers wisely and to exercise his judgement with discretion, common sense and sensitivity. Every police officer should understand that he holds his office on trust and by adhering to an established code of ethics he not only increases his professionalism but also ensures that this trust is not betrayed.

4　Police Discretion

Police discretion has long been the subject of considerable discussion and criticism particularly by those who genuinely believe that the independence of the police and their apparent lack of accountability lead to arbitrary decisions which cannot be challenged openly. The principle of independence and accountability is discussed later[1] but the importance of discretion lies in the fact that it covers a wide area of police activity which is often unregulated. Although much is left to the good sense, training and judgement of the individual officer, the discretion at play is far from absolute and is qualified by a number of factors and conditions which require careful analysis.

Discretion is an integral part of the criminal justice system though this is not always recognised or admitted. The sensitivity surrounding police discretion is the fact that it is the police who invariably decide who enters the criminal justice process whether by summons or arrest. Those who are not subjected to formal proceedings may be referred for informal action or no action may be taken at all. Decisions are often made in circumstances which are not amenable to scrutiny even by supervisory officers and it is crucial that this 'low visibility' area is recognised and principles established which regulate the exercise of this discretion.

It is a sad commentary on the level of police training in this country that discretion, so crucial to the police role, was never considered in the initial stages of training as a subject which could be taught formally or one which was amenable to scientific analysis. It was assumed that the practical application of discretion could be learned on the street from colleagues and supervisors. To the young police officer his training will certainly assist him to identify breaches of the law and he is often expected to enforce it rigidly in order to gain practical experience. It is often only after experiencing adverse public reaction to over-zealous enforcement that the officer realises that the maxim 'the law is the law' can only be a basis for determining his course of action. It can

63

provide no justification for eroding the public's confidence in the police and the way in which they exercise their judgement.

Discretion can be regarded, therefore, as another element of the fundamental principle of 'consent and balance'. Lord Scarman drew attention to the conflict which could arise between the duty of the police to maintain order and their duty to enforce the law. He emphasised that the successful solution of the conflict lay first in the priority to be given to the maintenance of public order and, secondly, in the constant and common-sense exercise of discretion. He said that the exercise of discretion lay at the heart of the policing function and it was well recognised that successful policing depended on the exercise of discretion in how the law was enforced.

> The good reputation of the police as a force depends upon the skill and judgement which policemen display in the particular circumstances of the cases and incidents which they are required to handle. Discretion is the art of suiting action to particular circumstances. It is the policeman's daily task.[2]

This suggests that discretion is an art which can only be acquired by developing practical skills but the difficulty lies in ensuring that officers not only develop such skills but are advised by supervisory officers who, themselves, have developed the proper skills associated with correct police practice. As long ago as 1929 the difficulty facing the inexperienced officer was described as follows.

> (He) must encounter many matters of much difficulty upon which he must decide on the instant – matters calling for tact, judgement, knowledge of the law and of his duties, and for decision of character. . . . The law and his knowledge of duty must be in his head, upon which he can alone rely to do the right thing at the right time.[3]

The young officer is often confused by the apparent conflict between his sworn duty to discharge his duties impartially and the notion that he can choose between enforcing the law in one situation but not in another. This is not to admit that differing standards of enforcement are to be applied. Lord Scarman pointed out that the law extended to all and should be applied firmly and fairly, but it should also be applied sensitively. He said that the existence of discretion, which the law had always recognised, enabled the police to act with sensitivity as well as firmly and fairly.[4]

It is quite obvious that it would be impossible to enforce all breaches of the law in all situations since this would fail to take into account any special circumstances in particular cases, quite apart from placing an intolerable burden on the courts. It is recognised, therefore, that the police operate a policy of selective enforcement based on fairness and reasonableness. This does not conflict with any established principle of legality and the rule of law since these are dependent on public respect for the law and its institutions and a policy of enforcement which clearly did not agree with the public's notion of fairness would soon erode respect for the law and the police who enforce it.

Imprecise terms such as 'selective enforcement' fail to explain who selects or by what criteria the selection is made. It is the officer on the street who is the key figure and his actions are governed by a number of considerations which require careful analysis. His actions will invariably involve several questions which he must ask himself:

1 Do I have a duty (moral or legal) to intervene?
2 Has an offence known to the criminal law been committed?
3 Has an offender been identified?
4 Do I deal with the matter informally or formally?
5 If formally, do I arrest or report for summons?

Analysed in this way, the issue seems a comparatively simple one but it must be remembered that quite often the officer is obliged to exercise his judgement spontaneously in a situation where there may well be stress on both sides. Furthermore, there may be doubts about the nature of the offence, the nature of the evidence against the offender and whether to arrest or not.

His initial involvement often depends on whether he detects the offence himself or whether he receives a report from a member of the public. In the latter situation, his discretion is fettered by the natural public expectation that he will deal with the offence and the offender. He cannot neglect his duty since this would be a matter for discipline yet his discretion may be influenced by the views of the complainant and discretion might still come into play at a later stage when the matter is referred to higher authority to prosecute. In trivial breaches of the law, the officer may find that he can take informal action with the agreement of the person reporting the matter but care must be taken to ensure that local enforcement policies are not affected.

An officer can also find himself in some doubt where a report is received from a member of the public who, while anxious to provoke some police response to a situation, is reluctant to become involved personally by giving evidence of the offence. The officer must also be careful to avoid being used to resolve petty disputes between neighbours and he must recognise at an early stage that allegations of offences arising from domestic disputes will quite often be withdrawn in the cold light of morning and formal action should be reserved for serious cases supported by written statements. These practical issues are not to be found in any textbooks and experience is often the best teacher but from a professional point of view, there should be clear guidelines laid down so that police action is regulated in similar situations and some degree of consistency is achieved.

The first issue an officer must apply his mind to is the nature of the offence itself. Invariably, his training will enable him to establish what offence has been or is being committed. In the case of regulatory offences involving road traffic law, the offences are absolute and no mental element (mens rea) is necessary to prove the offence. In a later chapter[5] it is suggested that such offences should not be included within the scope of the criminal law since persons committing minor traffic offences would not regard themselves as criminals and often take exception to the formal procedures associated with reporting offenders to which they are subjected. In the case of such traffic offences, there is considerable scope for individual discretion since some officers may choose to ignore the offence or to deal with it informally. Most police forces issue some guidance to officers as to minor offences which might normally attract a verbal caution at the time and even where offenders are reported, enforcement policies often include the issue of written cautions in appropriate cases.[6]

Personality factors may also come into play. In Chapter 5 on sense and sensitivity, it is suggested that the manner in which an officer approaches an incident will often dictate the course of events. Incivility will often provoke hostility and rational judgement then gives way to precipitate action. Officers acting under any form of stress may not always act in a rational manner and it is important that these factors are taken into account in assessing the justification of their actions. The young woman motorist is likely to attract more sympathy and consideration than a scruffy, abusive and objectionable youth on a motor cycle. The danger of stereotyping individuals is well recognised yet it previously formed no part of basic police training. Other aspects such as attitudes, communication skills, the avoidance of prejudice – not only racial prejudice – were also largely ignored yet the interaction between the police officer and the offender or suspected offender will affect the manner in which the officer exercises his discretion. It is easy to pass these off as human factors which cannot be regulated but it is now more widely accepted that the way in which an officer responds can be studied, evaluated and, above all, can be incorporated into initial training programmes.

The guiding principle of any enforcement policy must be fairness and openness. This often manifests itself in publicity campaigns where the police issues warnings of special measures to deal with particular problems. Typical instances are drink/driving offences during the Christmas period or the setting up of radar traps on certain roads to combat excessive speeding. Such measures usually attract public support since the purpose behind such campaigns is to reduce the number of deaths and injuries arising from accidents. Publicity with regard to special enforcement policies will also have a deterrent effect and act as a preventive measure in appropriate cases but this must always be supported by the capacity to enforce the law where necessary.

The principle of fairness may be in doubt in cases such as speeding where many offenders feel they have been picked on while others, who to their knowledge were also committing an offence, were not stopped. It is not always easy to rationalise the situation but it must be accepted that many motorists are committing offences every day of the year and face the risk of prosecution if detected. Fairness becomes an issue when offenders who are detected are dealt with differently and it is in order to avoid any inconsistency that prosecution policies are adopted at force level. In such cases, offences arising from any special enforcement measures are considered together in order that the question of prosecution can be decided on an equitable basis. This notion of fairness also extends to other areas of prosecution and is often overlooked as an essential ingredient of any criminal *justice* process.

Openness with regard to prosecution and enforcement policies has not always been a major issue in this country although Lord Scarman's Report touched on the question of police operations to tackle crime in sensitive areas. The problem facing the police at Brixton was street crime on an unacceptable scale and a saturation operation was mounted to combat street robberies or 'muggings'. The operation required the use of 'stop and search' procedures and Lord Scarman acknowledged that although some operations to prevent or defeat crime must plainly remain secret, others required the support and approval of the local community if they were to be successful. Street crime operations which involved 'stop and search' procedures would be bound to inconvenience, and might well embarrass or annoy, innocent people. He emphasised that there was a clear need for the local community to understand what the police were going to do and why.[7]

It must be said that this was a new approach to the question of police discretion and the suggestion that local community leaders should have been consulted before the police operation was mounted was regarded by many as a classic case of being wise after the event. Saturation policing in troublesome areas had been a feature of police operations in inner city areas for years and there was nothing to suggest that the presence of a large number of police in a high crime area was other than welcomed – except by those committing the crime!

Lord Scarman questioned the efficacy of such operations on the basis that there was no evidence that street crime diminished and the problem might only be transferred elsewhere.[8] With hindsight, local consultation might well have revealed that social tension existed but it is surely unfair to criticise the police commanders for lack of wisdom and judgement in a situation where their police experience dictated that a saturation operation was necessary and should be mounted. Before the Brixton disorders, there would have been many police commanders who would have regarded consultation with local community leaders beforehand as a danger to the success of the operation and an intrusion upon their independence of judgement as police officers.[9]

In the context of police discretion, the consultative machinery advocated by Lord Scarman,[10] whether voluntary or statutory, may well influence policy considerations with regard to law enforcement. The Report of Lord Scarman tended to ignore the existing local consultation and liaison which was already well established in many areas. The discretion to allocate police resources to deal with particular local crime patterns is well established and demonstrates that the police already have the capacity to identify and respond to local problems.

Difficulties arise, however, with police discretion in those areas of the criminal law which are affected by public morality for it is often difficult to assess the boundaries of public indignation or public tolerance. This is not a new problem in this country and the laws relating to drug abuse, homosexuality, prostitution, gambling and drinking have often formed the basis for challenging whether the criminal law should be used for enforcing morals. There are early examples in American history of the difficulties facing the police in trying to enforce unpopular laws relating to Sunday observance and prohibition. Unpopular laws are the responsibility of the legislature but enforcement is a matter for the police and it would be unwise for the police to embark on a policy of enforcement in those areas which might provoke an adverse reaction from the public.

The criminal law, itself, includes a recognised moral content which all people would accept as representing a common standard of morality in society. Such acts as murder, rape, violence and stealing would be included but difficulties might rise in obtaining common agreement over offences such as bigamy, incest or sexual offences between consenting juveniles. Incest did not reach the statute book until 1908. Attempted suicide remained a criminal offence until 1961. Social values change and the police must remain sensitive to clear expressions of public opinion on moral issues.

The Wolfenden Committee's Report in 1957[11] sought to define the function of the criminal law and it was concluded that its function was to preserve public order and decency, to protect the citizen from what is offensive or injurious, and to provide sufficient safeguards against exploitation and corruption of others. It also emphasised that there remained a realm of private morality which was not the law's business. It has been recognised by some American commentators that the criminal law is often used for social objectives instead of controlling criminal activity. Offences often come to light but no action is taken. It is suggested that some laws 'survive in order to satisfy moral objections to established modes of conduct. They are unenforced because we want to continue our conduct and unrepealed because we want to preserve our morals'.[12]

American research has also shown that the enforcement of laws involving moral issues such as prostitution, gambling, and drunkenness is affected by the police officer's perception of what the community's values are. Research was carried out among police officers in New Jersey and it was found that the police response was inclined towards taking some action rather than no action at all but that informal action was preferred to prosecution. There was a clear sensitivity to community attitudes, beliefs and expectations and the reaction of the police was governed not so much by a legal definition of what should be done as by a personal value judgement of the situation. Police action was determined by a judgement of what they were expected to do in each case.[13]

It should be stressed that the nature of community life in America and the relationship of the police to that community often makes it easier for public attitudes, beliefs and expectations to be determined. American history is a history of plural societies following mass immigration and it could be said that we are still adjusting to the notion of a plural society in this country. Some immigrant communities are not yet fully integrated and in changing societies, often characterised by plural religious and moral values, it is often difficult to identify acceptable or deviant behaviour and social attitudes towards morality.

Nevertheless, where a chief officer of police adopts a moral stance in relation to selective enforcement, he is on difficult ground. In 1968 a case of some significance was brought by Mr Raymond Blackburn against the Commissioner of the Metropolitan Police and an order of mandamus was sought from the High Court to direct the Commissioner to enforce the laws relating to gaming.[14] The application was withdrawn following an undertaking to the court that the policy would be revoked but Lord Denning commented,

I hold it to be the duty . . . of every Chief Constable to enforce the law of the land. He must decide whether or not suspected persons are to be prosecuted; and, if need be, bring the prosecution or see that it is brought. . . . he is not the servant of anyone save of the law itself. The responsibility of law enforcement lies on him. He is answerable to the law and to the law alone.[15]

It has been suggested that these remarks were *obiter dicta* and that the true *ratio decidendi* of the case was that the obligation on a chief officer to enforce the law was subject to judicial control and that some enforcement policies could be regarded as improper (for example an instruction not to prosecute any person for stealing goods worth less than £100). On the other hand, it was established that the mere existence of a policy of non-prosecution could not lead to an assumption that there was a breach of the recognised duty to enforce the law. It is clear that had the application not been withdrawn, the Commissioner's decision not to enforce the gaming laws could have been judicially controlled by an order of mandamus.

The real problem associated with the Commissioner's enforcement policy on gaming was that it effectively stopped observations and investigations into illegal gaming at a time when immense gambling empires were emerging bringing 'grave social evils' in their train together with 'protection rackets, crimes of violence and widespread corruption'. Another factor was that the enforcement policy was contrary to a clear intention by Parliament, as expressed in recent Acts of 1960 and 1963, to protect society against the evils which would follow from the exploitation of gaming. Although the moral force behind gaming legislation was apparent, the court took the view that comparable policies in relation to other laws on moral issues, such as sexual offences between teenagers, could be justified where the law concerned was not recent and legislative intent had become blurred by an identified change in morality.

The Commissioner could not rely on the uncertainty of the law as a reason for non-enforcement although Lord Denning rightly referred to the fact that, 'The niceties of drafting and the refinements of interpretation have led to uncertainties in the law itself. This has discouraged the police from keeping observation and taking action.'

While this case tended to support the independence of chief officers with regard to enforcement policies, it did suggest that the Court of Appeal's real objection to the Commissioner's stated enforcement policy on gaming was that it was not an exercise of discretion but an abdication of discretion altogether. Edmund

Davies LJ. took the view that an order of mandamus was 'designed simply and solely to ensure that the police do not abdicate, in consequence of a policy decision, their functions as law enforcement officers'.[16]

Four years later, Mr Blackburn again sought an order of mandamus against the Commissioner directing him to enforce the law on pornography. The order was refused and, in dismissing the appeal, Lord Denning again referred to the limitations of the law as a reason for police inaction.

> The cause of the ineffectiveness lies with the system and the framework in which the police have to operate. The Obscene Publications Act 1959 does not provide a sound foundation. It fails to provide a satisfactory test of obscenity, and it allows a defence of public good which has got out of hand. . . . If the people of this country want pornography stamped out, the legislature must amend the . . . Act *. . .* so as to make it strike unmistakably at pornography, and it must define the powers and duties of the police so as to enable them to take effective measures for the purpose.

Another member of the Court of Appeal was not impressed by the Commissioner's view that pornography was not a high priority in relation to enforcement.

> The Commissioner may be right when he says that at present pornography causes less public unease than most other breaches of the law. In my judgement, it is high time that its gravity was appreciated by the public. It cannot fail . . . to affect the morals and the moral outlook of many people, and in particular of the young and impressionable.[17]

The efforts by Mr Blackburn to try to impose some judicial control over the discretion exercised by chief officers of police, although unsuccessful, did provide a useful indicator that this aspect of police discretion was not absolute but qualified by a number of considerations not the least of which was the need to maintain public confidence in the police. 'If there are grounds for suspecting that a grave social evil is being allowed to flourish unchecked because of a set policy of inaction decided upon by a pusillanimous police force, public confidence must inevitably be gravely undermined.'

The dilemma in making policy decisions on enforcement is that inaction may undermine public confidence and other action may, as at Brixton, provoke public hostility. The real difficulty with selective enforcement is the danger that professional judgement on moral issues may become an expression of personal moral values which are out of step with public morality. If there is less public unease about pornography, the judiciary do not share that view. More recently, the Lord Chief Justice spoke of the imitative effect of the huge increase in the sale of pornography which, because of the rarefication and recondite type of sexual behaviour which now accompanied crime, made crime almost inevitable. He referred to glossy imports which percolated through various shops and found their way into the hands of young people with inevitable serious results.[18]

In 1977, the Chief Constable of Greater Manchester made a determined effort to root out pornography. He launched numerous vice squad raids in a drive to clear the city streets of pornography and prostitution. He was left in no doubt by the flood of letters he received that he was acting with public support and approval. He stated that most people had said it was long overdue and that he had responded in a sensible way to public complaint and abhorrence at what they had seen around them.

The control of a chief constable's exercise of discretion in law enforcement is really a question of accountability and he clearly owes a duty to the law itself and a duty to the public to enforce it. This duty carries with it a correlative right for the law (through the courts) and for the public (through elected representatives) to ensure that the law is enforced in appropriate cases, but this is difficult to achieve without undermining the principle of independence, particularly from political interference.

To the officer in the street, these issues may seem rather remote but he is the person who enforces the law whether on his own initiative or in accordance with stated enforcement policies. A particular concern is that, if unregulated, the constable is the person who decides the effective scope of the criminal law by determining the limits of law enforcement.[19] One American commentator[20] has raised important questions on discretion and asks whether the individual police officer, despite his own value system, should be delegated broad powers of discretion or whether procedures should be designed in order to translate community values into rules and regulations for the individual officer. He also asks whether the purpose of the criminal law in imposing minimum standards of human behaviour on society should be undermined by the practice of discretion and whether its effect can be evaluated.

The writer concludes:

> The ultimate answer is that the police should not be delegated discretion . . . but . . . the police should operate in an atmosphere which exhorts and commands them to invoke impartially all criminal laws within the bounds of full enforcement. If a criminal law is ill-advised, poorly defined, or too costly to enforce, efforts by the police to achieve full enforcement should generate pressures for legislative action. Responsibility for the enactment, amendment and repeal of the criminal law will not, then, be abandoned to the whim of each police officer or department, but retained where it belongs in a democracy – with elected representatives.

This idealistic view recognises that full enforcement is, 'neither workable nor humane nor humanly possible under present conditions' but the writer suggests that the ultimate objective should be to enact new criminal codes which would remove obsolete offences.

Doubts have also been expressed as to whether the police should allow trivial offences to go unpunished where the offender is able to supply information to assist in the detection of more serious offences. Although the arrest and conviction of the main offender may seem to be the end which justifies the means, there is considerable disquiet over the extent of police activity in this area. This raises the same questions as to whether a policy of non-enforcement in exchange for information undermines the retributive or deterrent function of the criminal law.

The effect of some enforcement policies on other criminal activity is also an area which has not been evaluated. If, for example, a campaign was waged against drug suppliers would this lead to supply problems and increase the price of the drug on the streets? Would this, in turn, lead to an increase in crime to finance further purchases? Is it right that these should be relevant considerations and is it possible to anticipate the likely effects of non-enforcement policies?

What does seem to emerge is that it is preferable for enforcement policies to be based on full enforcement using the individual officer's judgement and complaints by individual members of the public as a regulating factor. The latter will certainly be an indicator of public reaction to certain types of offences and whether the right balance of law enforcement is being achieved. As already observed, the individual officer's judgement is a variable factor but one which is amenable to formal training and which can be regulated.

This judgement is seldom more exposed to critical analysis than in the decision to arrest an offender. The law has always recognised the discretionary aspect of arrest and many statutes contain express powers of arrest which include the word 'may' and the power is often qualified by further conditions such as 'reasonable suspicion' and failure to give name and address. To a police officer, an arrest is a familiar occurrence but it should never be overlooked that for the person being arrested, it is often a traumatic and unfamiliar experience. The power to arrest therefore should not be exercised lightly but wisely and only where necessary. Arbitrary arrest with little or no suspicion is the hallmark of oppression and it is right that the exercise of the power to arrest should be open to close scrutiny and subjected to adequate safeguards for the individual.

In a free society, the freedom of the individual is paramount and this freedom should be protected from all arbitrary action and abuse. The police officer's powers are defined by law but where these powers are qualified by a requirement of 'reasonable suspicion' problems of interpretation arise and the decision to arrest can often involve a fine degree of professional judgement. This judgement may be based on common police practice and guidance from supervisory officers but it is not surprising that officers may sometimes take precipitate action in good faith as a practical measure during the investigative process.

The courts have tried to issue guidelines but the legality and justification of an arrest is not usually in issue once a prisoner is before the court on a substantive charge and a conviction follows. Lord Devlin, in one of the few cases on the issue, offers some guidance on the exercise of discretion when arresting on 'reasonable suspicion'.

The circumstances of the case should be such that a reasonable man acting without passion or prejudice would fairly have suspected the person of having committed the offence. It is important that hasty or ill-advised police action should be avoided. If on the other hand the police hesitate too long to arrest a person when they have proper and sufficient ground for suspicion against him, they may lose the opportunity of arresting him or may enable him to destroy evidence.[21]

The officer's decision is not assisted by the fact that this case also reiterated the practical consideration that the degree of suspicion to justify an arrest is not necessarily the same degree required to support a charge. Suspicion is a starting point leading to a prima facie case being established and can be based on matters which might be inadmissible as evidence to support the charge.

Lord Devlin's test of a 'reasonable man acting without passion or prejudice' suffers from the same difficulty as 'the man on the Clapham omnibus' in civil law or, in America, 'the man who takes the magazines at home, and in the evening pushes the lawn mower in his shirt sleeves'. A better view, perhaps, is that 'the reasonable man' is a fiction – he is the personification of the court and jury's social judgement'.[22] There is some validity in this view but in the sphere of police activities, it is difficult to impart to a court or to a jury, the professional considerations which apply to the police practice of arresting on suspicion.

This was recognised by the Advisory Committee on Drug Dependence when considering the criteria for 'reasonable grounds' for arrest and search.[23] They referred to an unwritten code which was familiar to every police officer, but much less familiar to the public. The Committee attempted to set out the criteria for 'reasonable suspicion' but added,

To any such list must be added the essential fund of common sense, training and experience which every police officer is deemed to possess in some measure and without the exercise of which he may find himself in trouble with his superior officers. It is this critical element which makes a statutory definition of 'reasonable grounds' so difficult.

More recently, the Royal Commission on Criminal Procedure

endorsed this view when considering the clarification of police powers. They recognised that the principal safeguard would be found in the requirement for, and stricter application of, the criterion for reasonable suspicion. Some had complained that the police interpreted this too loosely and that in normal circumstances, the court did not test it. This increased the risk of random stops.

> We acknowledge the risk that the criterion could be loosely interpreted and have considered the possibility of trying to find some agreed standards which could form the grounds of reasonable suspicion and could be set out in a statute or in a code of practice. Like others before us we have concluded that the variety of circumstances that would have to be covered makes this impracticable.[24]

The Royal Commission were also anxious to ensure as far as possible that the criterion of reasonable suspicion was not devalued and they recommended that coercive powers should be placed on a statutory basis which would enshrine the general principles for their availability and exercise, and spell out safeguards for the application of each power. In addition to the application of the criterion of suspicion on reasonable grounds, the decision to use any particular power and the reasons for that decision should, where practicable, be recorded at the time so that its exercise could be reviewed after the event.[25]

It is clear that the Royal Commission felt that in the important area of arrest and detention, the existing controls on police discretion were inadequate and they were responding to a genuine feeling of public disquiet that the police were abusing their powers in some situations. They were concerned over the suggestion that too many people were being arrested and subsequently not prosecuted. Similarly, some were not being told the grounds for arrest while others were being arrested solely for questioning where there were no reasonable grounds for suspecting them of any offence.[26]

The Royal Commission felt that many of the problems stemmed from a lack of clarity with regard to powers of arrest which made the task of the police more difficult and the citizen uncertain of his rights. Evidence given to the Commission suggested that a wider use of summons would enable people to be brought before the court without being deprived of their liberty and research showed that there were marked differences between police forces in the use of summons and arrest for indictable offences. In 1976, for example, four forces, including the Metropolitan Police, had only used summons procedure in 1 per cent or less of indictable cases against adults and in seven other forces 40 per cent or more of such persons had been proceeded against by this means.[27]

This demonstrated a wide variation in the exercise of the discretionary power of arrest and in order to regulate this discretion the Royal Commission decided to adopt a 'necessity principle'[28] whereby an arrest would be justified for one or more of the following reasons:

1. The person's unwillingness to identify himself so that a summons may be served on him.
2. The need to prevent the continuation or repetition of that offence.
3. The need to protect the arrested person himself or other persons or property.
4. The need to secure or preserve evidence of or relating to that offence or to obtain such evidence from the suspect by questioning him.
5. The likelihood of the person failing to appear at court to answer any charge made against him.

It was felt that this 'necessity principle' should apply to the question of continued detention in custody after arrest and the Commission proposed to put these criteria on a statutory basis so that the police were obliged to take them into account in order to justify the initial arrest and subsequent detention. The intention was to limit detention upon arrest to those cases where it was absolutely necessary. This would regulate the use of the discretionary powers of arrest and would provide a good, working guide for the police officer.

The Commission recognised the difficulties facing the police officer on the street and said that they had considered whether these criteria should be applied statutorily at the point of arrest so that an arrest made and detention continued when one or more of them did not apply would be rendered unlawful. They thought it would not be practicable to place so stringent a requirement upon police officers in the street. Often decisions would have to be taken urgently and in the midst of disturbances or otherwise confused situations. The earliest point at which the criteria should be applied by statute was when the arrested person was brought to the police station.[29]

The application of these criteria to continued detention would ensure that the officer in charge of the station could only lawfully detain a person when it was essential to do so and the Commission thought that, in applying these criteria, he should have regard to the nature and seriousness of the offence, the nature, age and circumstances of the suspect and the nature of the investigation that is required.[30] It was emphasised that it was not always necessary to detain a person in custody in order to question him or to carry out other enquiries and the practice of questioning juveniles at home should be encouraged.

One of the main purposes behind the Royal Commission's comprehensive study of criminal procedure was to identify those areas of police activity which were largely unregulated and consequently open to abuse. Their recommendations, after implementation, were intended to allay public disquiet and also maintain the confidence of the public in the police. The requirement that the reasons for decisions on detention should be recorded was seen as the basis for greater accountability after the event. Similarly, by clarifying many existing police powers and providing a code of practice to regulate interviews by the police, it would be easier to test the lawfulness and propriety of police action. This, in turn, would assist the police by standardising practices which, hitherto, had varied considerably across the country and left many decisions in the discretionary process unchallengeable.

The obvious concern was that the proposals of the Royal Commission would inhibit or frustrate the police in their investigations into crime but the Commission were clearly alive to the real practical difficulties facing the police officer on the street. A rationalisation in police powers to stop and search was recommended which would extend the existing power to search for stolen goods on reasonable suspicion to the whole of England and Wales. Powers to arrest without warrant would be placed on a consistent footing and where a person was seen committing an offence for which no power to arrest without warrant existed, he could nevertheless be arrested if he positively refused to give his name and address.

As summarised in the chapter on police ethics, the standards applied by the Royal Commission when evaluating the existing police procedures included fairness and openness in order that any proposals made would enable the police to exercise their discretion in such a way as to command public confidence. Fairness is very much associated with justice and an ethical basis for police action. Openness has long been recognised as one of the best ways of controlling the exercise of police discretion.

Kenneth Culp Davis[31] analysed the nature of discretion and concluded that 'Discretionary power can be either too broad or too narrow. When it is too broad, justice may suffer from arbitrariness or inequality. When it is too narrow, justice may suffer from insufficient individualising.' By this he means that discretion is essential to any system of justice and 'The proper goal is to eliminate unnecessary discretionary power, not to eliminate *all* discretionary power.'

Davis bases his conclusions on the view that 'Where law ends, discretion begins and the exercise of discretion may mean either beneficience or tyranny, either justice or injustice, either reasonableness or arbitrariness.' He poses the question of how to regularise discretion so that a higher quality of justice is achieved. His answer lies in the structure of discretion and he distinguishes this from confining discretion. 'The purpose of confining is to keep discretionary power within designated boundaries. . . . The purpose of structuring is to control the manner of the exercise of discretionary power within the boundaries . . .'.

Although Davis was considering discretion as it applied to the whole process of criminal and administrative law, his instrument for structuring discretion was one of the standards applied by the Royal Commission in formulating their proposals – openness. He maintains that:

> The seven instruments that are most useful in the structuring of discretionary power are open plans, open policy statements, open rules, open findings, open reasons, open precedents and fair informal procedure. The reason for repeating the word 'open' is a powerful one: Openness is the natural enemy of arbitrariness and a natural ally in the fight against injustice.[32]

Davis refers to the common law tradition of openness and reinforces the point with support from Jeremy Bentham that

'Without publicity, all other checks are insufficient: in comparison of publicity, all other checks are of small account.'[33] Similarly, he adds the view of Mr Justice Brandeis that 'Sunlight is said to be the best of disinfectants; electric light, the most efficient policeman.'[34]

In a later article, Davis deals exclusively with police discretion in the United States.[35] With the wide variation in police practice in America, the demand for greater structuring of discretion is considerable since justice should share common ground. Davis comments 'Police discretion is absolutely essential. It cannot be eliminated. Any effort to eliminate it would be ridiculous. But *unnecessary* police discretion can and should be controlled – can and should be properly confined, structured and checked.'

The use of the exclusionary rule to regulate police action was described in the chapter on police ethics but Davis feels that this is of limited value as this only refers to some 3 per cent of police activity. He favours a wide use of judicial control whereby rules governing police discretion would be subject to judicial review. Davis concludes that the police are in a better position than the justices to formulate the rules but judicial review of matters such as enforcement policies would command public support. He also advocates an extension of tort liability as a means of regulating discretion by providing a remedy for those subjected to unlawful police action. In England, following the Police Act 1964, a person can sue the Chief Constable for the wrongful acts of constables but in the United States it is not always possible to claim against the state or local government and persons aggrieved are often deterred from seeking a remedy.

Davis' views, though based on American research and practice, do emphasise, however, the fundamental issues surrounding police discretion and the varied views from writers on both sides of the Atlantic have served to highlight the difficulties of regulating it. One English contributor to the debate on discretion, drawing on research in both America and England contrasts the different approaches to policing in city and rural areas and concludes that the police invariably interpret their role and exercise their discretion in direct response to community definitions. In city areas with a heterogeneous population community expectations were difficult to define and the only identifiable consensus centred on the control of crime. In rural areas, however, with a relatively homogeneous community, there was a wider consensus of the police role and concern over other problems requiring police intervention and it was easier for the police to identify what was expected of them.[36]

Bottomley summarises the difficulties facing the police officer in determining his role and when and how to act.

> Unfortunately, the problems of contemporary policing are firmly located in the urban environment of our big cities where neither community nor consensus on 'law and order' are readily identifiable. The police are thus increasingly pushed back onto their own internal resources and assessments of aims and efficiency. At the same time there are internal pressures from police management towards greater 'professionalism' so that the officer on the beat has the unenviable task of interpreting the mandate of law and order for himself with little guidance from the community he is policing, while attempting to reconcile this with the operational requirements of emergent police professionalism.[37]

In Chapter 3 on ethics, the influence of police professionalism has already been considered and there should, in theory, be little difficulty in an officer reconciling his role *vis-à-vis* the community and his own professionalism since the latter is based on wide ethical considerations which provide a yardstick against which his actions can be measured not only by himself but by the public generally. The practical difficulties are largely created by the limitations in an officer's early training which concentrates on the law and police powers without providing the necessary social and ethical basis which places the exercise of these powers into their proper perspective.[38] Since an officer's subsequent advice and guidance is derived principally from immediate supervisors who themselves have developed in a climate which did not encourage any consideration of their social role, the theoretical benefits are submerged among the practical aspects of policing.

Furthermore, there is a tendency to regard social considerations as a softening of the police approach towards hardened criminals and serious crime. The concern of the public over serious crime and disorder should dispel that notion but the real danger, as indicated by the Brixton disorders, lies in an inflexible approach which limits the capacity of the individual officer to recognise that some matters require the full rigour of the law and other objectives can be achieved and issues resolved without invoking the full exercise of his powers.

This may be regarded as common sense but common to whom? How can community objectives and expectations be assessed particularly where heterogeneous communities consist of a wide diversification of culture, religion and public morality. The difficulties were succinctly put by one politician who commented that he 'did not believe in the collective wisdom of individual ignorance'. The defect in asserting that policing should be dictated by the expectations of the community lies in the fact that these expectations vary widely and can rarely be effectively rationalised.

It is equally defective to assert that there can never be any issues on policing which can be referred for local consultation. Current practice clearly suggests otherwise. Although this touches on the wider issues of independence and accountability the fact remains that the police cannot operate in isolation using their accountability to the law as the only justification for their actions. Provided their actions are regulated by professional considerations of conduct and policy; provided their actions are lawful and in accordance with the principles of fairness and openness, there should be no reason for public concern.

There remains a further area of police discretion which has long been the subject of critical comment – the prosecution of offenders. While this is obviously linked to the discretion on enforcement, it does represent a secondary stage in the enforcement process which enables the police officer's initial action to be reviewed and a reasoned decision made with regard to instituting proceedings against the accused. The procedure differs in arrest cases since if the arrest has been made in proper circumstances, such as 'reasonable suspicion', the officer in charge of the police station to which the person is brought is obliged to enquire into the matter and make a decision as to whether a charge should be preferred or not.[39]

In certain circumstances, the matter may be deferred and the person released on condition that he reports back to the police station at a later date.[40] The charge against the person may be refused if it is found on enquiry that there is no evidence to substantiate a charge against him. The practice has developed whereby some offenders, particularly the young, the elderly or infirm, are released and the matter dealt with by way of the summons procedure. This raises the obvious question of why the individual should have been arrested in the first place but such cases invariably arise where the alleged offender has been arrested or detained by a third party and the police are then required to attend and intervene.

Proceedings by way of summons is the alternative to arrest and, having regard to the Royal Commission's adoption of a 'necessity principle' for arrest,[41] the method of dealing with the majority of offenders where an arrest is unnecessary. It is clear that the Royal Commission felt that the summons procedure should be more widely used since it enabled a person to appear before a court without losing his liberty.[42] It also provided an opportunity for the evidence to be weighed and tested and other relevant considerations to be taken into account before a final decision was made.

The discretion as to whether to arrest or proceed by summons has already been touched on but the importance of arrest in relation to prosecution lies in the fact that the arrest invariably puts the whole machinery of prosecution into action. The Royal Commission on Criminal Procedure referred to the importance of the initial decision that is taken by the police officer on the street or by the officer who first receives a report of a supposed offence from a member of the public. 'That officer's discretion, although it is not entirely unfettered, controls the input to the prosecution system.'[43]

In arrest cases, where a prima facie case is established, an alleged offender is then charged and the process is then set in motion for the person to appear before a court. Although in many cases, there is ample evidence on which a charge can be based, a prima facie case literally means 'a first view or consideration' of the issue and there may occasionally be secondary considerations which could affect the nature of the charge or even confirm the innocence of the accused.

Those who criticise the discretion of the police to prosecute favour a separation of the investigator and the prosecutor. The latter, it is felt, should be able to take an objective view of the evidence and it was argued before the Royal Commission on Criminal Procedure that the investigator (the police), by virtue of his function, was incapable of making a dispassionate decision.[44] Other critics, such as Bottomley, suggest that once an arrest has been made the police apply a 'presumption of guilt' which, 'pervades much police behaviour in the processes of interrogation, charging and preparing the case for trial. For the police to work without such a presumption would tend to undermine the justification, in their own minds, for the earlier decision to arrest'.[45]

This view tends to suggest that the police are incapable of acting in the interests of justice and fails to take into account the supervisory safeguards which often result in charges being refused where an arrest on 'reasonable suspicion' cannot be justified in the first instance. Nevertheless, it would indeed be surprising if the police, charged with the responsibility of investigating crime, did not consider it their duty to obtain all relevant admissible evidence to put before the court in order to rebut the 'presumption of innocence'. If this means that the police operate with a 'presumption of guilt' then the view may be valid but that does not necessarily mean that the presumption is irrebuttable if the police find evidence in favour of an accused. To suggest otherwise is to adopt a cynical view of police practice and efficiency.

The Royal Commission commented:

It may perhaps be true that the investigator is psychologically committed to a belief in the guilt of the suspect and is therefore incapable of making a dispassionate decision on whether or not to prosecute. . . . It may be equally true that lawyers who spend their professional lives working in a prosecution agency become just as committed to securing convictions as police officers are said to do.[46]

This suggests that whoever has the responsibility to evaluate the evidence and conduct prosecutions will naturally proceed on the basis that the initial police action was justified since if it was not justified on the evidence available to the arresting or reporting officer, the normal police supervisory safeguards would have precluded any prosecution being commenced. The main criticism of the police role in both investigating the offence and prosecuting the offender is that any decision made by the police to prosecute is not amenable to independent review. There is no openness. There is no formal record required of the reasons why prosecutions are or are not taken in particular cases.

Because police decision making in respect of prosecutions is 'closed' as distinct from 'open' it is wrongly concluded that arbitrary decisions are taken or that no set criteria are being applied or, at least, consistently applied. The same criticism is made of other police action especially that surrounding arrest and detention, but in this area the Royal Commission, in recommending additional safeguards against arbitrary police action, were influenced by evidence that arbitrary arrests and abuse of powers did occur.

This was at the initial stages of the investigatory process but no such justification could be found for recommending changes in the prosecuting function which, it was urged, should be removed from the police and placed with an independent legally qualified prosecutor. It was argued that there was no strong evidence that the police had fulfilled their functions as prosecutors less than adequately. Removing the decision from them would, therefore, be an arbitrary and doctrinaire expression of the public's lack of confidence in their competence and integrity and would be likely to be damaging to morale and hence to their effectiveness in law enforcement.[47]

The view was also expressed that the police were in a more appropriate position to take into account other factors such as wider public attitudes and public order considerations. The Commission also explored the possibility that the function could be divided with the prosecutor deciding the legal and evidentiary issues and the police deciding the issues relating to social and policy grounds. After a full and comprehensive review of all the issues, the Commission favoured a division of functions between the police and the prosecutor.

The Commission's objective was to secure that after a clearly defined point during the preparation of a case for trial and during its presentation at trial someone with legal qualifications made the necessary decisions to ensure that only properly selected, prepared and presented cases came before the court for disposal. The aim was to achieve this without affecting the quality of police investigation and preliminary case preparation and without increasing delays.[48]

In countries such as the United States and Scotland, the Commission noted that the decision to bring an offender before the court lay not with the police but with an independent, legally qualified official[49] who took into account all the issues whether evidentiary or related to the wider public interest. In both systems it was found difficult to draw a line between the function of the

investigator and the prosecutor. The Commission were favour-
ably influenced by the systems studied in parts of Canada and this
led them to conclude that it was difficult to dissociate the conduct
of the investigation from the decision to prosecute. The majority
of decisions to prosecute did not present problems of legal
complexity and although the critical decisions had to be police
decisions, a genuinely independent and legally qualified person
was required to conduct the prosecution once the initial decision
to proceed had been taken.[50]

The Royal Commission rejected the suggestion that the
decision to prosecute should be removed entirely from the police
and drew attention to the fact that the decision to prosecute was
invariably a long series of decisions which involved enquiries into
whether a criminal offence had been committed and whether
there was sufficient evidence to support a prima facie case. It
would be impractical for an independent prosecutor to intervene
in these enquiries before the police had determined these
matters.[51]

It was felt that the dividing line between the function of the
police and the independent prosecutor should be as clearly drawn
as possible and the Royal Commission concluded that the police
should be left with the complete responsibility for investigating
offences and for making the initial decision as to whether the
matter should be placed before a court or not. This would also
enable the police to continue to exercise their discretion as to
whether to caution a person as an alternative to proceedings.[52]
The Royal Commission also believed that the formal cautioning
procedure should be placed on a statutory basis and criteria
should be established to remove the present wide variation in
police cautioning policies.[53]

The effect of these recommendations on police practice would
be that their discretion would become qualified rather than
absolute. The existing referrals to the Director of Public Prosecutions already qualify police discretion in a limited number of cases
but subsequent proposals for a national prosecution system
envisaged that the final decision to prosecute would not lie with
the police.

The apparent need for a 'genuinely independent' person to
assume this role suggested that the police discretion to prosecute
was unregulated and, by implication, unfair. Moreover, it failed
to take into account the historical and constitutional basis on

which the police had always undertaken prosecutions. The introduction of the police system in the nineteenth century merely provided a formal structure for the previous practice whereby the constable brought, in theory, a private prosecution. The basis for retaining the decision to prosecute as an element of police independence relied on the constitutional position of the constable who acted under the authority of the Crown and was accountable to the law rather than to central or local government.

This aspect of police independence and accountability is developed further in Chapter 8 but the proposal to establish an independent prosecution system, was essentially a decision against principle. The duty on the police to enforce the law is clear and has judicial support. It is difficult to divorce the nature of enforcement from the ultimate decision to prosecute. In the *Blackburn* case, Lord Denning saw prosecution as synonymous with enforcement.[54]

This erosion of police discretion by an independent prosecution system may well be seen as an unnecessary and expensive adjustment to a system of justice which already had the confidence of the majority of the public. It is the discretion of the police, coupled with the professional integrity which independence demands, that breeds this confidence. The argument that any change would be 'an arbitrary and doctrinaire expression of the public's lack of confidence' is difficult to resist. It would indeed be a touch of irony if a decision to regulate alleged arbitrary decisions by the police was, itself, an arbitrary one.

Important decisions by the police to prosecute are, at present, seldom made in isolation. Current practice reflects full consultation between the police and prosecuting solicitors over decisions, a practice which allows public interest, based on local considerations, to be taken into account. Guidelines on prosecutions also regulate the decision to prosecute and can reflect national considerations and achieve greater consistency.

The whole emphasis of the Royal Commission's detailed examination of the decision to prosecute was placed on fairness, openness and accountability and their recommendations to place it on a statutory footing arose from the need to develop agreed and consistent criteria for the exercise of the prosecutor's discretion. The Commission adopted the same test as that applied by the Director of Public Prosecutions; that there should be a reasonable prospect of conviction before going ahead with a prosecution.

Even when this test is satisfied, other factors should be taken into account such as:

1. the staleness of the offence;
2. the youth or age of the offender;
3. any mental illness or stress affecting the offender;
4. the attitude of the victim;
5. the relationship of the victim to the offender.

It was conceded that it would be impossible to provide an exhaustive list but an attempt should be made under the auspices of the Director of Public Prosecutions to develop and promulgate throughout the police and prosecution services criteria for the exercise of the discretion to prosecute.[55] The suggested criteria would be applied on the basis that an offence known to the law had been committed and that there was evidence to support the accusation. The Commission stressed that the further down the path towards prosecution a case had travelled, the more important it became that whoever took the decision to continue proceedings should be satisfied that there was evidence by which the offence could, if necessary be proved.[56]

It is interesting to note the Commission's view that the minimum standard of evidence to justify a prosecution goes beyond the existence of a prima facie case and they adopted the Director of Public Prosecution's test of whether there is a reasonable prospect of conviction. This requires the prosecutor to make a judgement, a prediction, as to whether the evidence is likely to be sufficient.

> Someone should not be put on trial if it can be predicted, with some confidence, that he is more likely than not to be acquitted. . . . We therefore suggest that the prosecutor should have to satisfy himself that there is a reasonable prospect of conviction before going ahead with a prosecution.[57]

From a jurisprudential view, this ingredient of 'predictability' of what the courts will acccept or do has been the basis for asserting that the nature of law does not consist of rules but predictions. 'Rule-scepticism' claims that statutes are not laws but merely sources of law and that the law consists simply of the decisions of courts and the prediction of them.[58] This raises again the crucial role of the police in the criminal justice process as it has already been suggested that the discretion of the individual police officer and his decision to arrest or report offenders determines the limits of law enforcement. Indeed, it has been suggested that the police officer, in effect, makes the law.

> It is the individual policeman's responsibility to decide if and how the law should be applied, and he searches for the proper combination of cues on which to base his decision . . . he, in effect, makes the law; it is his decision that establishes the boundary between legal and illegal.[59]

This is really too narrow a view since the police officer's decision is not always an individual one and is often affected by other factors such as a report from a member of the public or directions of a senior officer, but it does emphasise the responsibility of the individual officer to act fairly and reasonably. To do otherwise will not only undermine his own authority but, more crucially, will undermine the authority of the law itself. Any measures, therefore, which help to regulate and control an officer's discretion must be seen as beneficial to both the individual and society itself.

The proposals by the Royal Commission on Criminal Procedure were intended to provide statutory criteria concerning the arrest and detention of alleged offenders and whether they should be cautioned or prosecuted. In this way decisions could be measured against the relevant criteria and this 'openness' would remove any doubt in a particular case that the police had acted in an unfair or arbitrary manner.

One final point should be made. The general movement towards more openness and fairness tends to suggest that because the decision making process involved with police discretion has been too 'closed' it has been unfair. It has been unfair in that there have been variations in prosecution policies across the country and in the justification for arrests but unfairness carries with it a suggestion of injustice, discrimination and abuse on a wide scale. The nature of the police role and procedures does not readily admit a convenient system of external supervision and this closed environment has frustrated any protracted research into police procedures with the result that the suggestion that the police have 'something to hide' is difficult to refute. Such a suggestion places too little emphasis on the high degree of professional judgement and responsibility shown by so many officers in their daily duties.

What must be recognised is that police officers are ordinary family men and women who are charged with a responsibility to act on behalf of the community. They are individuals with different personalities, attitudes and capacity for judgement who are dealing regularly with a wide cross section of the public who themselves are blessed with mixed qualities and attitudes towards the law and those responsible for enforcing it. It is impossible to legislate for all situations but it is possible to regulate discretion by providing an officer in the early stages of his training with practical guidelines based on the wider professional aspects of his role. This underlying concept of professionalism includes a recognition that a course of action can be analysed and studied to such a degree that officers know and understand the reasons why they should act in particular situations.

Once this is understood, the officer can then make a conscious effort to regulate his own conduct and make a balanced judgement on how he should act. In this way, officers can be trained to act consistently so as to minimise the risk of abuse and arbitrary action. This, in turn, should enable the public to retain their confidence and trust in the police system.

5   Sense and Sensitivity

Lord Scarman's summary of the principle of 'consent and balance' referred to in the chapter on 'Discretion' stressed the importance of the commonsense exercise of discretion and that the existence of discretion enables the police to act with sensitivity as well as firmly and fairly.[1] This suggests that a discussion on sense and sensitivity is merely an extension of the views expressed on discretion and it is true that discretion includes the application of common sense and sensitivity. Sensitivity, like discretion, operates at different levels and the sensitivity referred to by Lord Scarman was in respect of enforcement policies and policing generally. His comments were directed at those officers who are responsible for operational policies and the style of policing to be adopted in particular areas.

Reference was made to the evidence submitted by the Chief Constable of Greater Manchester which emphasised the importance of sensitivity at street level.

> It is right that the integrity of the law should be preserved but the means to achieve this can be different. In short, therefore, it is patently obvious that when various social pressures and tensions exist within any particular community, it is imperative that police officers on duty in the area adopt a sensible and sensitive approach.[2]

Policing with sense and sensitivity, therefore, was revived as an essential element of effective policing but it is clear from the reference to the traditional principle enunciated by Sir Charles Rowan[3] that this was not being offered as something new arising from the ashes of Brixton. The events at Brixton were merely a grim reminder that where social pressures and tensions exist within a community, the police must adjust their policies and this must be reflected in their methods of policing. The problem lies in ensuring that the policies set out at command level are implemented at street level. This is the distinction between theory and practice.

In dealing with discretion, it is suggested there should be more openness with regard to policing policies and it is clear that the events at Brixton highlighted the need for greater consultation with community leaders. This should ensure greater sensitivity and community involvement in policing policies but fails to take into account the crucial point that it is the individual officer on the street who carries the real burden of sensitive policing. Written orders and policies count for very little unless there is a wide commitment by police at all levels to ensure the policies are implemented in a sensible and sensitive way.

The responsibility placed on the shoulders of patrol officers when exercising discretion is often a difficult one and invariably involves a situation where the officer has to decide on a particular course of action. Having decided on a course of action, whether formal or informal, he effectively sets himself an objective which can be achieved in a number of ways. Sense and sensitivity is involved not only in deciding what to do in certain situations, but how to do it. There are several areas in which it is vital for the police officer to understand that although the insignificant daily incidents are familiar to him, contact with the police is an unfamiliar experience for many members of the public. The officer has to adapt to the individual and take his cue from the circumstances. He may have to display tact, good humour, tolerance, sympathy, compassion or patience. He will have to display self-discipline and even temper in the face of extreme provocation, yet still remain civil and courteous.

Any police officer will know how difficult it can be to measure up to this ideal but the price of misjudging the situation or the individual with whom he is dealing will often be complaint or criticism and this can soon undermine the reputation of the police and the officer's own confidence. Either way, the police service suffers and it is important that certain recurring aspects of police activity are analysed in order that officers are better able to anticipate difficulties and approach their duties with a wider appreciation of public expectation.

One of the greatest difficulties facing the young police officer is communication with the public. Effective communication is crucial to his role since it underlies his relationship with the public he serves. It is the first step towards mutual understanding and it has to be suitable and sufficient for breaking down a variety of barriers which may be placed in the officer's way. Communication can be verbal, written or merely gestures, expressions or body movements, and may involve contact with individuals or groups. It is so much a part of everyday life that little conscious thought is given to developing skills in communicating with others. This is due to the fact that in the ordinary course of events there is a mutual willingness to communicate and any defects are absorbed by the tolerance of the persons concerned. Provided the message is conveyed there is no reason to suppose that any difficulties exist. It is only when a police officer fails to take into account the particular circumstances or the peculiarities of the individual that he realises that effective communication is a skill which can be acquired.

If the communication process is analysed further, there are several factors which are of particular importance to the police officer in his relationship with the public. These factors are variable ones depending on the circumstances but it will be obvious that communication in a stressful situation will require greater skill than in a situation where no tension exists. In the latter situation, little difficulty should arise but factors such as appearance, manner of speech and loose language can often cause offence in the mildest of situations.

Common courtesy costs nothing yet it has the capacity to ease communication and establish mutual understanding. Everyone is entitled to be addressed in a polite manner whatever his status yet there are recurring examples of rudeness and discourtesy which give rise to complaint. The Police Complaints Board have referred to the inexperience of some young officers who do not always realise that a remark which may be acceptable among their contemporaries might be regarded as insolent or rude by an older member of the public.[4]

The Board also commented on thoughtless and insensitive conduct which gave rise to recurring complaints. These included unnecessary visits to a person's home at night and an unhelpful attitude towards the relatives of persons arrested.[5] In such situations, it is not difficult to understand the problems associated with communication. It is not necessarily the nature of what is said but the circumstances in which the conversation takes place.

It will be readily apparent that a police officer's daily duties involve him in the lives and problems of a wide cross section of society and his intervention often requires a high degree of sensitivity. The right attitude and the right words can overcome many difficulties and a police officer requires practice and training in order to develop the skills of communication. He should therefore be conscious of those factors which facilitate good communication. Many people seeking help from the police usually have a problem or crisis in their own lives and it is important that an officer develops the art of listening. Hearing is a physiological function but listening requires a degree of perception and understanding. This perception can take account of a variety of additional factors such as gestures and expressions since listening has a creative influence. The listener must understand what is being said since the police officer often requires to make a rapid appreciation of what is being reported. He must develop the art of perception by using his ears and eyes, asking only those questions which are necessary to clarify what is being said.

It was once remarked that you were given two ears and two eyes but only one mouth in order that you could hear and see twice as much as you speak. This may seem a contradiction in a discussion on communication but research has shown that in the ordinary communication process as little as 35 per cent of the social meaning of the situation is conveyed verbally and no less than 65 per cent is conveyed by non-verbal means such as appearance, gestures, posture, facial expression and voice tone.

Some police officers might view such conclusions with a little scepticism and even amusement but if they were to see themselves in action they would soon become aware of how some events are dictated by the appearance, gestures and expressions of themselves and others. A smart and presentable officer will promote confidence and respect whereas a slovenly or improperly dressed officer will often unconsciously cause others to lose respect and ignore what he has to say. This may be interpreted by the officer as an unwillingness to accept what he is saying and a barrier is thrown up between them.

The ordinary motorist may find himself confronted by an officer whose manner of approach, characterised by a searching physical examination of the vehicle, immediately makes effective communication difficult. Any hostile reaction to the officer is then remedied by an over-zealous enforcement of trivial offences connected with the vehicle. Research has indicated that a police officer's decision to report a motorist may often be due to the attitude of the offender. This attitude may be influenced by the nature of the offence, or a general attitude of hostility towards the officer or the police.[6] Decisions based on attitudes must be of doubtful validity and if these attitudes have been due to the officer's own appearance, behaviour or language, the value of a sensible and sensitive approach to enforcing traffic law is self-evident.

One of the most common discourtesies giving rise to complaint is that of disinterest. Many people put themselves to considerable inconvenience to report matters and often think twice before doing so. Trivial matters of little concern to the police may be important to the individual concerned. To treat such persons with disinterest is not only discourteous but is unacceptable in a profession which purports to care about ordinary people.

It has been found that many people are more concerned over local issues such as nuisances caused by neighbours, rowdy youths and excessive noise than they are about crime. It is important that police officers recognise that a proper response to comparatively trivial problems, even if it is confined to advice, can do much to reassure and assist the public. Follow-up visits to explain police action and the result of police enquiries are not only common courtesy but an indication of a proper interest in resolving sensitive disputes within the community.

Problems may arise with communication due to midunderstanding, often through ignorance, imprecise language or lack of information. In some circumstances, misunderstanding of police action may exist through rumours and it becomes necessary for the police to convey accurate information quickly in order to allay anxiety or reduce tension.[7]

Communication between the police and individuals or even whole communities can become strained by factors which create barriers and a study of records of complaints from the public would provide several examples of where the police officer or an individual has failed to recognise the existence of these barriers. In some areas, particularly multi-racial areas, cultural differences are often ignored. Different cultures often lead to different outlooks and values and for many years the police have received training in race relations which attempts to provide some education on cultural backgrounds of immigrant communities. Similarly, attempts have been made to describe the police role to these communities. It is often difficult to change attitudes but a mutual understanding of cultural differences has proved an effective aid to good communication.

A guiding rule for a police officer is to treat others as he himself would like to be treated. Provocative remarks or thoughtless comments can create difficulties which are so easily avoided. A police officer often has a delicate role to play in a confrontation situation. He is often in a privileged position since provocative remarks made to him will invariably provoke a response and formal police action. Derogatory comments such as 'pig' or 'fuzz' can often cause resentment among officers and they must realise that similar loose comments about individuals or groups can provoke similar hostility with no immediate remedy for the person who is offended.

The police occupy a unique place in society and sensible policing can only be achieved by each officer making a clear distinction between his own individual attitudes and those expected of him as a professional police officer. Personality traits should, where possible, be identified in an effort to eliminate incorrect attitudes or prejudices. This is a difficult area and corrective action is invariably taken only after a particular trait has come to notice during operational duty. Attitudes affect behaviour and there is no reason why professional attitudes cannot be included in an officer's initial training so that he realises that such matters as prejudice, stereotyping and bias must be eliminated and that his actions must be based on correct attitudes.

Prejudice has been defined as a vagrant opinion without any visible means of support. It is invariably linked with racial groups and is often based on mistaken beliefs or myths. It usually appears in the form of generalised statements which have the immediate attraction of supporting the view being advanced and, being generalisations, they are seldom capable of being refuted instantly.

The elimination of prejudice is of vital importance to the police officer since prejudice creates attitudes which manifest themselves in certain behaviour. Initially, there is a feeling of superiority which, in turn, leads to discrimination. This discrimination seeks justification in a feeling of superiority in that supposed inferior groups can be treated differently. Prejudice also involves proprietary claims and that members of the supposed superior group have a stronger claim to residential areas, employment, public office and other powerful positions. Prejudice also breeds fear and persons may become irrational.

The collective effect of these attitudes is a progressive pattern of behaviour towards the object of prejudice. The first phase involves conversation and derogatory comments and this may lead to avoidance or isolation. A simple example is a refusal to sit next to another and this may lead to more active behaviour designed to make life uncomfortable for the other person. This is the stage at which discrimination is apparent and the group or individual is subjected to social or other restrictions.

The next level of behaviour involves the use of physical violence against persons or damage to property. It is at this level that the worst manifestations of prejudice appear and it can equally be directed towards the police as by the police. It is often said that prejudice is blind in that it fails to take into account any particular qualities of the individual being subjected to prejudice. It is invariably directed towards a group irrespective of the individuals within the group and, paradoxically, the discrimination is itself indiscriminate.

To the police officer any suggestion of prejudice at any level should be resisted not only because it offends against the general principle of impartiality but does so on the basis of ignorance. Everyone has some prejudices to a greater or lesser degree and it is impossible to eliminate prejudice altogether but the police officer must recognise that his duty is to treat all persons equally and that he has no right to allow personal prejudice to influence his behaviour. To do so not only conflicts with the officer's professional image but may lead to the worst aspects of prejudicial behaviour.

The police officer, in performing his duties, will know that all people have differing views and attitudes towards a variety of matters and it is the dominant attitudes which will dictate a person's behaviour. In order to act with sense and sensitivity, an officer must take into account his own attitudes and those of the persons with whom he comes into contact. The International Association of Chief Police Officers have offered guidelines which give practical advice on the management of attitudes by police officers. They form the basis of many training manuals in America and are repeated here as an indispensable ingredient of effective policing.

1. An officer's private attitudes should not be permitted to influence his official decisions. He must strive for a high degree of objectivity in his work. In short, he should not make judgments on the basis of his own ideas of right and wrong or his likes and dislikes.

2. An officer should not become *personally* involved when making an arrest. He must not look upon a violation as a *personal affront*. It is a wrong against the state, the people, and not against him personally.

3. Nobody and nothing in the rules requires an officer to *like* the people he deals with. Similarly, and more important, nobody and nothing in the rules says he must *dislike* them. However, bear in mind that if people either see or believe that you dislike them, your contact will always be more difficult and less effective.

4. Do not permit people *to goad you* into showing anger. There is an old saying: He who angers you, conquers you.

5. *Try to show an attitude of neutrality and objectivity.* Let people see *that there is nothing personal* in what you are doing when your contact is of an adversary type; you are acting officially and according to the rules. An attitude of sympathy and human concern would, of course, be appropriate in a contact in which you are rendering a helpful service. By showing that there is nothing personal in your actions in an adversary contact, you will focus the hostility of the people on the system and not on you personally. This will also help you avoid charges of brutality, rudeness, or lack of courtesy.

Given these general guidelines, the police officer is better equipped to deal with the many situations he may have to face. Whatever preconceived ideas he may have had before joining the police service, he cannot escape the conclusion that the police profession is people-orientated and that he must become proficient at dealing with people. The principle of policing by consent is reinforced by the fact that police officers are appointed to serve the community and that the respect of the community has to be earned daily. The public expect much of their police and it is right this should be so, but the police role can often be a demanding one particularly at times of crisis.

Many police officers in America receive training in crisis intervention, a term which covers those incidents and events which commonly occur and which require the police to act with sensitivity. It may be crime, an accident or sudden death but the incident is characterised by intense psychological stress on the part of those immediately affected by the crisis. Officers can be trained to develop techniques in dealing with personal crises and an understanding of the difficulties involved can enable an officer to handle the incident effectively.

The police occupy a unique role in that they have the capacity to respond at any time of the day or night and it is this which often causes the public to contact the police at times of individual crisis. Traditionally, the police have always adopted a supportive role in situations where they have no legal duty to intervene. It is the public's expectation that help will always be available and the proper handling of crisis situations can do much to foster good relations between the police and the public. The police develop expertise in these recurring situations and a professional approach based on confidence, efficiency, sincerity and empathy can be so crucial in helping the individual to deal with the crisis.

The nature of policing often involves the police officer in apportioning blame in connection with certain incidents, but in the field of crisis intervention his immediate concern should be directed towards the plight of the individual and to providing immediate assistance. It is only too easy to confuse the helping and blaming roles so that the person in the centre of the crisis is made to feel guilty; that the incident could have been avoided or that the consequences might have been less serious. Such insensitivity frustrates the purpose for which the police were called in the first place and the police officer tries to control the situation in a positive way so that the individual concerned is reassured. This can often be achieved merely by emphasising that the person did the right thing by calling the police.

Decisive and positive action is often crucial in helping persons to overcome particular crises yet an inexperienced officer may feel there is little that he can do. Worse still, the action he takes, though intended to be supportive, may be taken without regard to the adverse effect of his actions. Inappropriate or insensitive comments within the hearing of the victim or relatives or unnecessary officiousness can often aggravate the situation.

Police training on crisis intervention is designed to ensure as far as possible that the person overcomes the immediate crisis and that continued support is available. Quite often, the victim of a crisis will be displaying verbal or physical signs of distress accompanied by indecision and a loss of confidence. Police action is intended to provide support at each phase so that the victim of the crisis can regain his dignity and respect and also regain his confidence. In some cases the very presence of the police can do much to inspire confidence among those present. If this is accompanied by a calm, courteous, sensitive and decisive approach, the police task of providing immediate support can be accomplished.

Certain principles can be applied to police action in those recurring situations which provoke stress and crisis. Death, whether expected or unexpected, often involves police intervention and many police officers try to remain emotionally detached from the situation they are dealing with. Young or inexperienced officers often have great difficulty in dealing with sudden death but nevertheless are expected to comfort the bereaved and deal efficiently with investigatory and administrative tasks. Even the most hardened officers are sometimes affected by a child death or the sight of severe injuries. In trying to suppress any overt reaction, the police officer may become too engrossed with administrative detail that he ignores his crucial role of support to the relatives. His response will also tend to vary according to the nature of the death and whether it has been due to natural causes, accident, suicide or homicide.

The officer may be faced with a cot death and distraught parents yet this is not far removed from death due to child neglect or abuse. He is expected to comfort the bereaved yet not close his mind to the possibility that the death was non-accidental. Such cases call for sensitive handling as even in genuine cot deaths the parents are plagued with guilt and self-recrimination. All deaths call for sympathetic and sensitive handling and no other situation calls for more understanding, help and support by the police officer involved.

Victims of crime also require support and help from the police and in many areas schemes have been introduced which provide a voluntary response from persons or organisations in the community. Such schemes provide a secondary level of support for a victim thereby releasing the police officer to continue with his investigation. It is still vital, however, for police officers to be fully aware of the psychological effect on the victim of crime since it will help him to understand certain attitudes and behaviour on the part of the victim. From a professional point of view, it enables the police officer to obtain the maximum amount of information which will assist in the investigation of the crime.

In America, the study of a victim's reaction to crime is referred to as victimology. Dr. Robert Flint has contributed much to the study of the initial response to victims and much of his work on the psychology of victims has provided the basis for police training in this important area.[8] It is essentially the application of psychological first aid and many of the suggestions in this chapter are an indication of the positive steps which a police officer can take to prevent a deepening of the trauma experienced by many victims of crime.

In England, very little attention is paid to the subject and again it seems that it is a subject which can be learned from colleagues during training on the street. Many would take the view that it is a matter which is not amenable to scientific treatment and that the common sense approach – whatever that means – is to make enquiries into the crime without too much regard to the effect of the crime on the victim. There are recognised phases of reaction to crime and a victim may exhibit signs of denial, blame, anger or resolve.

Denial is a psychological process which refuses to face reality and some victims of crime may be unable to accept what has happened. A typical example is the person who walks around a car park looking for his vehicle which has been stolen. In other cases, victims may accept that a crime has occurred but make a conscious attempt to control themselves and give the impression that the experience has had little impact on them. This type of behaviour is often associated with women victims of crime and there is often an emotional response when kindness and consideration are shown.

A victim may also suffer a guilt complex over the fact that the crime was committed. The sensitive police officer will refrain from making a victim feel he or she is to blame for the crime having been committed. It can be of little comfort to a person to be told that he should have made his house more secure or locked valuables out of sight. Similarly, victims of rape do not need reminding that they should not have dressed provocatively or drunk too much since they are already painfully aware of their misfortune. Victims usually wish to avoid any suggestion of blame for the crime and may often accuse others indiscriminately in order to shift the blame. Even the police may not be blameless if it is thought they should have prevented the crime in the first place. A strong sense of guilt may even prevent the person reporting the crime at all.

Anger may follow blame and may be directed at others indiscriminately or at the police. Surprisingly, victims may be reluctant to voice their anger at the criminal and adopt an understanding stance. This is usually an indication of the fear to which the victim has been subjected and is commonly found in crimes involving personal violence. Where anger is shown towards the police themselves they should not become involved in an attempt to defend their position.

A victim of crime needs considerable support especially from the police who are often in a better position than most to provide it. They need help in a practical way such as advice on additional security measures or submitting a claim for insurance. There is a clear need for them to face reality, to place blame and direct anger towards the criminal and to overcome the crisis with firm determination. The degree of sensitivity required in dealing with victims of crime is often not fully appreciated by police officers usually for no other reason than that crime is a common occurrence to them and they often fail to put themselves in the place of the victim.

This is well illustrated by offences of burglary which cause particular distress to victims owing to the fact that their privacy has been invaded. Quite often, the police officer and the victim view the crime differently. The police officer, being familiar with crime, may treat the matter too lightly because he is aware of far more serious crimes, that insurance will invariably cover the loss and that the possibility of detecting the crime is remote. The victim, on the other hand, is greatly affected by the burglary and regards it as a serious personal experience. All the symptoms of shock, denial, blame and anger can be present and there may be personal items of property stolen which are of great sentimental value. No insurance can compensate for the loss and the victim expects the police to be successful in detecting the crime and recovering the property.

This apparent conflict requires the police officer to be sensitive to the feelings of others. Although the officer may fail to understand the victim's plight, being insignificant compared with his own experiences of crime and violence the officer must guard against appearing indifferent or disinterested and realise that the victim requires reassurance, support and advice. He must strike a balance between his own experience and the victim's inexperience. It would be too optimistic and, indeed, palpably false, to promise that the property will be recovered and, similarly, it would be unhelpful to suggest that the victim will never see the property again.[9]

In crimes where personal violence has been used, the police officer must display particular sensitivity in dealing with the victim. In rape cases, the experienced investigating officer avoids aggressive questioning and patiently obtains information from the victim in such a way that any suggestion of blame or shame is avoided. The home may be the best place to question a victim unless the offence was committed there or there is an expressed wish that relatives should not be told. On the other hand, the victim may need support and help in explaining the crime to her family. It is common practice for a woman officer to be present at an interview but it has been found advisable to have a male officer present as an understanding and sympathetic male officer can often help the victim overcome an understandable aversion to men following the offence.

Child victims of sexual offences also require an investigating officer to adopt a sympathetic approach to the investigation. The attitude of the parents and possible feelings of guilt can often hamper an enquiry and lead to important information being suppressed. Such a crime invariably produces a crisis in the whole family of the victim and affects relationships even between sister and brother. An understanding of these difficulties is essential to a police officer in order to fulfil his role as the first line of support to victims of crime.

In his study of the psychology of victims, Flint deals with the role of the police officer in helping victims to overcome the psychological shock they have experienced. He emphasises that

> They (victims) also need the information and psychological support which a police officer can supply to help them develop secure expectations about the future. They need help to regain their feelings about the future. They need help to regain their feelings of self respect and control over their environment.

It is in this situation that the technique of good communication referred to earlier in this chapter is so essential. Good listening techniques can be developed so as to reassure the victim and inspire confidence. A police officer can judge by the victim's responses whether he is too near or too far away. The greater the distance, the greater the degree of formality. Some victims may be glad of a reassuring hand or arm although victims of violent crimes might feel threatened by such actions. Similarly, a victim should be spoken to in a soft, slow voice so as to indicate patience and concern.

Other techniques include 'active listening' whereby questions seeking clarification can indicate that the officer understands what is being said and attaches importance to it. The occasional summary of what has been said can indicate interest and understanding while periods of silence after questions allow the victim more time to recollect facts.

This confusion amongst victims can also be eased by statements from the police officer which may appear obvious but, nevertheless, are reassuring, such as 'I can see this has been an upsetting experience for you.' The use of 'I feel' or 'I think' creates a personalised statement and indicates personal concern for the victim. Personal expressions of concern can do much to ease the situation and to help minimise the harmful effects of the crime. It allows the victim to regain composure, dignity and self-respect. Even a simple request to enter the home is sufficient to help the victim re-establish some control over the situation and supporting comments to the effect that the victim did the right thing can restore confidence.

The elderly deserve special consideration, particularly as victims of crime, since age invariably brings with it an increasing awareness of vulnerability and helplessness. The extent of crime is often more imagined than real although the fear created by the media, who often give undue prominence to the sensational aspects of crime, is real enough. Anything which can dispel this fear of imminent crime should be actively pursued and the police officer should go out of his way to reassure the elderly as often as possible.[10] Many elderly people are genuinely frightened and tend to ring the police more often. A sympathetic and reassuring officer can do much to assist even though the matter reported proves to be trivial or non-existent.

The problems of the elderly are invariably brought about by social isolation. Men and women who have worked hard often in responsible positions suddenly find themselves isolated by retirement which becomes more acute as they grow older. Many, through immobility or ill-health, are often reduced to mere observers. Some lose contact with their children and have intense feelings of loneliness. This loneliness is compounded by the death of a spouse or friend particularly where there has been a high degree of dependence.

The police can play an important role in helping the elderly to retain their dignity, self-respect and sense of purpose. Regular patrolling in residential areas where the elderly live can do much to reassure them and whenever the police have occasion to visit the elderly for any reason, they should understand the plight of many elderly people and adopt a full supportive role. In many cases, the police may need to refer the elderly to the various social agencies which exist but the social role of the police officer should not be minimised or discounted. The police cannot work in isolation; they have a responsibility to the society they serve and the traditional nature of policing embraces this notion of assisting the public rather than oppressing them.

It was perhaps an indication of the inadequate training given to the British police officer that it required a serious breakdown of law and order at Brixton for sensitive policing to become a matter of concern. The respect and acceptability of the police by the public has to be earned every day by every officer and there are countless examples of members of the public expressing their appreciation of police action which far outweigh the number of complaints against the police. Every person who comes into contact with the police carries away an impression of the police which is either favourable or unfavourable. This may reinforce his attitude towards the police or cause him to change it.

The benefits arising from fostering good relationships with the public hardly need to be stressed but policing is a difficult function and police officers themselves are often under stress when dealing with certain incidents and situations. This is particularly so where the officer is a perfectionist and allows frustration to affect his performance. Stress is a condition which is often disguised and officers, seemingly quite confident, can be suffering mentally and physically for no other reason than that they are anxious to perform well. This concern is not helped when other pressures, internally from supervisors or externally by domestic or personal issues, intervene. Every situation in which an officer gets involved has the potential to become a stressful one. Where a police officer is involved in a stressful situation it is difficult for him to apply the principles of sensible and sensitive policing if he, himself, is acting under stress. His performance will suffer and the end result will invariably be unsatisfactory, which may also add to his stress.

Stress, itself, can either have a positive or negative aspect. The positive aspect can amount to an improvement in performance and lead to a capacity to meet challenges and overcome obstacles. The negative aspect includes fear, frustration and worry. Stress depends on personality factors and the individual's capacity to cope with the situation he faces. The same situation may produce fear in one or exhilaration in the other. If there is a positive reaction to the situation, the degree of stress is reduced but a negative reaction can result in behavioural and emotional symptoms.

The professional police officer tries to develop his skill and knowledge so that his general level of confidence and competence reduces the negative aspect of stress and enables him to perform more effectively. Where stress induces extremes of behaviour, whether for the police officer or others he is dealing with, aggressiveness, hostility or indifference can arise and this often prevents the officer from controlling the situation. Such symptoms are indications that the person concerned is unable to cope and although in the short term it can be regarded as a natural reaction to stress, the real danger lies in the fact that when these reactions recur regularly they become integrated in the personality. Aggressiveness and hostility are common characteristics of persons being arrested and any police officer will be familiar with them. It is important to recognise that the same indications from police officers are not only unacceptable in terms of self-discipline but also give a clear warning that the officer is unable to cope.

The pressures on the ordinary police officer are numerous and can come from outside sources or from within the police service itself. It is hard to preach sensible and sensitive policing to officers who are exposed to the problems of urban policing, especially the now notorious inner city areas. The great majority of the public fully support the police function but at street level it seems that some officers have lost the skill of communication and traditional policing methods have been dressed up as 'community policing' and offered as a new concept designed to win back support and confidence which should never have been lost in the first place.

Public attitudes have changed as people have become increasingly aware of the limitations on police powers. Some young persons, in particular, no longer have respect for authority generally and know that they can often be abusive and uncooperative without incurring formal police action. Other persons, who do become the subject of formal action, may make vindictive complaints against the police and, although most complaints are proved to be groundless or unsubstantiated, the effect on the officer complained of can be considerable. He will often be under stress while the complaint is investigated and it may well affect his attitude towards his duties. He often finds it hard to understand why a senior officer should devote more time to a complaint against him than he himself is able to devote to allegations of serious crime.

In addition to the obvious stress and difficulties in dealing with street incidents, an officer can often find the judicial process another source of stress and dissatisfaction. It is difficult to reconcile the fact that criminals escape conviction by a technicality or defect in procedure when the very nature of justice implies fairness. The officer sees the worst aspect of crime and the distress caused to victims and where long weeks or even months have been spent investigating the crime, it can be demoralising to see the person responsible escape conviction.

It is also difficult to reconcile justice with a system which adjusts its policies on economic rather than social grounds. If a criminal must be imprisoned in the public interest the availability of suitable accommodation should not be a relevant consideration. It is true that the criminal justice system should not be the concern of the police since there should be a clear division of function but the collective effect of anomalies in the system does tend to shape attitudes. Police officers may try to compensate for deficiencies in the system but this can be counter-productive and is often at the expense of sensible and sensitive policing.

Policing, therefore, involves a continuous relationship with the public at all levels and a mutual understanding of each other's difficulties. Sensitivity implies an awareness of the other person's situation so that the police officer can act as effectively as possible. The public do not expect the police to be super-human and they know that police officers are subjected to exactly the same type of difficulties as other members of the public. The difference lies in the fact that police conduct has to be judged on a higher level consistent with the concept of professionalism. If the police take no account of social considerations, human weakness and human vulnerability and rely on the law alone to give them authority, then they have not grasped the essential nature of the police role.

I have already referred to the well-worn concept of community policing which formed part of the evidence before Lord Scarman. He took the view that some senior police officers felt that community policing ignored the harsh realities of crime in the inner cities and that what is good for a country market town is not necessarily appropriate to a deprived inner city area.[11] It was felt that this contrast between 'hard' and 'soft' policing was too simplistic and that policing was too complex to be considered in this way.

Successful policing involves a flexible approach to policing requirements in each area and the police are expected to use their professional judgement to determine what method of policing is appropriate in the circumstances. The lesson from the Brixton disorders is that community relations form an essential element in policing by consent and that the feelings of the community on particular policing issues cannot be ignored. This is nothing new but is merely a re-statement of the traditional policing role.

Sensitivity to the individual widens to sensitivity towards the public at large for the police must judge local expectations and opinions in formulating local policing policies.

Sense and sensitivity, therefore, is an integral part of policing with consent whether in connection with general policing policies in particular areas or confined to particular action by an individual constable. It is a natural support for the proper exercise of discretion and ethical standards of conduct which elevates mere policing into the realms of professionalism. This is not to suggest that policing cannot at times be firm as well as fair. Firm and positive action is often called for in situations where the public would expect the police to respond.

Such positive action often involves the use of force and it is appropriate that the principle of minimum use of force should be recognised as one of the distinguishing features of traditional policing in this country. Recent experiences in the field of public order suggest that the police may be in danger of blurring the principle of minimum force and adopting methods which demonstrate a capacity for using more force than is necessary. This important shift of emphasis requires further examination.

6   The Principle of Minimum Force

The principle which embodies the minimum use of force became firmly established with the creation of the modern police system in 1829. The circumstances of crime and disorder which provided the impetus for police reform during the latter half of the eighteenth century and the early nineteenth century have already been described. It was essentially a conflict between those who viewed the imposition of a police force on the population as an assault on liberty and those who recognised that the establishment of a police system was the only way in which liberty could be preserved. This conflict arose largely because of public ignorance of the way in which the law operated within society and, particularly, of the way in which the law could be enforced. Lawlessness and disorder had prompted more restrictive laws and severe penalties but these had had little impact on the problem.

Gradually, it became more widely recognised that the law itself was an insufficient guarantee of individual liberty unless it was supplemented by an effective means of enforcing it. Historically, the army had always represented the ultimate coercive element in society whether the threat to the established system was from internal or external sources. The notion that 'might was right' was the basis on which force was used to secure compliance, but the failure to control the widespread crime and disorder led to fierce debate and proposals for reform of the criminal law. It was not readily apparent to influential people at the time that the failure of the law to contain crime and disorder was not due to the nature of the law but the means of enforcing it. It was against this background that the measures taken by the Fielding brothers, Colquhoun and Peel assumed such significance.[1]

In the early part of the nineteenth century the army had been used to suppress the Luddite riots and the 'Peterloo Massacres' at

Manchester in 1819 again saw the army deployed against the rioting working classes. There is little doubt that this latter event which involved the death of eleven people and 400 injured caused great resentment, shock and open hostility towards the use of naked force. It proved a turning point in public opinion which shifted in favour of some system of organised police.

It had long been the considered view of many people that there was something inherently wrong in using armed force in order to suppress the civilian population. The army operated on the principle of maximum force and were inevitably linked with central government and oppressive conduct. As such, it had no relationship with the criminal law nor acted under its authority. The force used to quell the mob was blind, arbitrary and oppressive.

The ultimate failure of the army to provide an acceptable means of enforcing the law and restoring order lay in the fact that the force used to achieve its objectives was excessive. Consequently, although it acted with the approval of government, on whom responsibility for law and order rested, it did not act with the approval of the people.

The lessons learned from the disorders in the early part of the nineteenth century were not lost on Peel who consciously organised and developed his new police in a way which sought to win public approval. He was clearly influenced by events in France and elsewhere and he understood the general abhorrence to any form of policing which reflected the characteristics of the French model. In seeking public approval, Peel was determined to avoid any suggestion that the new police were to be used in an arbitrary way by central government since he recognised that the liberty of the individual was highly valued.

It is doubtful if Peel could have envisaged how successful his new police were to prove. Peel's conception and vision embraced the principle of prevention and this applied not only to crime but to disorder as well. The coercive element was replaced by a persuasive approach which recognised that objectives could be achieved in many situations without resorting to the use of force. Thus the first instructions issued to the police embraced the principle of minimum force which was expressed as follows. 'By the use of tact and good humour the public can normally be induced to comply with directions and thus the necessity for using force, with its possible disapproval, is avoided.'

Any fears that the new police would operate in similar fashion to the military model in Europe were soon dispelled as the new police officers emerged on to the streets, dressed in a civilian style uniform of broad brimmed hats and blue tail-coats. They were armed with only a wooden truncheon and there must have been serious doubts among observers at the time as to whether this new police could be termed a 'force' at all. In the early months, they faced considerable public hostility and politically motivated mobs sought to discredit the police on the basis that liberty was threatened. False allegations of brutality and contrived confrontations failed to provoke a reaction from the new police and the value of good discipline was much in evidence.

In the formative years, hostility and distrust continued but Rowan and Mayne, the first two commissioners, were determined to persist with this new style of policing. The riots which preceded the Reform Bill in 1831–32 proved a further test of the resilience of the police and the response of the government was not to alter the nature of the new police and give them additional arms but the provision of statutory measures to create special constables. There was to be no departure from the principle of minimum force and a notable incident in Cold Bath Fields at Clerkenwell in 1833 witnessed the dispersal of an armed mob by a small well-disciplined body of police armed only with truncheons. There were no civilian casualties but one police officer was stabbed to death. Public opinion turned in favour of the police who had shown great restraint in difficult circumstances. The mob had been dispersed without recourse to the military and the pattern had been set for an acceptable and effective method of dealing with riots. The restraining influence of a large number of police officers under firm discipline and control became the traditional method of dealing with subsequent riots and disorder.

The principle of minimum force developed empirically from early practice and eventually embraced the whole area of coercive powers. This was a natural progression since the principle, once established, gave its validity to a wider area of police activity characterised by the need for the police to achieve lawful objectives by the use of force. The use of such force had long been established under the common law and the wisdom of Peel in retaining the common law powers of a constable for the new police ensured that it was acceptable to those traditionalists who doubted the emergence of the new police and who might have regarded it as a creature of government and a threat to personal liberty.

It had long been established that the use of force in making an arrest could only be justified if the accused resisted or attempted to escape. Historically, the ordinary people were vested with the same common law powers and there were legal restraints on excessive use of force. The police could be held accountable for their actions and this was an important basis for eventual public support and approval for the way in which the new police operated.

It was this blend of traditional common law powers and the new concepts of prevention and persuasion which gave the police its unique character. The influence of the common law was referred to in the debate on the Criminal Code Commission Bill of 1879 when it was said:

> We take one great principle of the common law to be that although it sanctions the defence of a man's person, liberty and property against illegal violence and permits the use of force to prevent crimes, to preserve the public peace and to bring offenders to justice, yet all this is subject to the restriction that the force used is necessary; that is, that the mischief sought to be prevented could not be prevented by less violent means; and that the mischief done by, or which might reasonably be anticipated from, the force used is not disproportioned to the injury or mischief which it is intended to prevent.

The common law powers relating to the use of force were eventually incorporated in the Criminal Law Act of 1967 and the Criminal Law Revision Committee's report which preceded this Act rationalised the old distinction between felonies and misdemeanours and the powers available to constables and private individuals. The Act expressly referred to the fact that the new provisions replaced the common law rules on the use of justifiable force.[2] It provided that any person could use such force as was reasonable in the circumstances in the prevention of crime, in effecting or assisting in the lawful arrest of offenders or suspected offenders or of persons unlawfully at large.[3]

By vesting these powers in the ordinary citizen, the Act re-affirmed the common law duty of all persons to prevent crime and assist those responsible for enforcing it. As with many other powers associated with arrest, the fact that the police were given no additional powers above the ordinary citizen emphasised the unique character of the British police system and ensured that police action in exercising these powers attracted popular support.

In recommending that the old common law powers should be simplified and given statutory force, the Criminal Law Revision Committee did not provide any clear guidelines as to what might constitute 'reasonable force'. They merely commented that the court would take into account all the circumstances including the nature and degree of the force used, the seriousness of the end to be prevented and the possibility of preventing it by other means.

The word 'reasonable' suffers from the same difficulties of interpretation which have plagued the courts, both civil and criminal, for many years.[4] Attempts to provide satisfactory criteria to meet every situation have proved largely futile and there is a scarcity of judicial comment on the matter. If the use of force by the police is considered in the wider context of police powers and the use of force to enter premises, judicial guidance as to the nature of 'force' and the justification for its use can prove helpful.[5] Lord Justice Donaldson, in summarising his view of the use of force to gain entry, a power confined to the police by the Criminal Law Act 1967,[6] defined 'force' as the application of energy to any obstacle the police might meet with a view to removing it.[7] He stressed that the force used had to be justified and this principle of justification embraced a further principle of necessity.

> The first hurdle which he (the police officer) will have to overcome in justifying force will be by providing an answer to the question, 'Why did not you ask to be allowed in?' That 'an Englishman's home is his castle' is perhaps a trite expression, but it has immense importance. Anybody who seeks to enter by force has a very severe burden to displace. . . . The statute says that force can be used 'if need be'. All I am saying is that those words are of immense weight and importance and if the question arises, 'Was it necessary?' the constable will have to prove that it really was necessary before he will be able to justify an entry by force . . .[8]

If the constable carries a heavy burden of proof to justify entry into premises by force, then, *a fortiori*, he has a heavier burden to discharge with regard to the use of force against the person. It is for this reason that the criteria for the application of lawful force should be fully understood and clearly stated. There are many difficulties associated with such terms as 'reasonable', 'necessary' or 'justifiable' not the least of which is whether the test is subjective or objective. The very word 'reasonable' suggests a rational basis for police action which can be tested objectively. Although powers are often expressed in subjective terms, an officer cannot rely on an unreasonable degree of force to justify his actions.

The boundaries between the application of lawful force and unlawful force are invariably blurred since the recurring situations of arrest involve such varying degrees of force as to render many questions as to its reasonableness difficult to answer. In some situations, a mild degree of force could be unreasonable yet in other situations it might be necessary to use considerable force in order to restrain a person who is being arrested. The arresting officer is often placed in a difficult position for it is necessary for him to achieve his objective by the arrest and the force applied is in direct relation to the resistance offered.

There is a growing tendency for persons to resist arrest by assaulting the arresting officer and in situations where persons are arrested for drunkenness and public order offences, the officer is conscious of achieving his objective with the minimum of disruption to the general public. The belief that the majority of such persons will 'come quietly' is not always confirmed and arrests in the public arena are invariably subjected to critical public comment and scrutiny. The arresting officer alone will have to determine the degree of force to be used and he is fully liable at criminal and civil law if excessive force is employed. If excessive force is used, it will result in his having to account for his actions, not only in law, but also under disciplinary regulations which prohibit the use of unnecessary violence during the course of his duty.

The principle of minimum force, therefore, is highly valued and is at the core of the relationship between the police and the public. The restraint shown by police officers in many situations is evidence of the principle in practice. It is fundamental to public approval of police action and complements the principle of policing by consent. It is always necessary to show that the degree of force used was only sufficient to achieve the objective and the degree of force used must be commensurate with the resistance offered. Force must not be resorted to if the objective can be achieved by other means.

It would be wrong to imagine that the police are required to use force on a regular basis as a means of achieving their objectives and great emphasis has been placed on the term 'service' to distinguish it from the widely recognised use of 'police force'. The very concept of law enforcement, however, implies the ultimate use of force and this is often a compelling reason why so many persons co-operate with the police on arrest and others willingly comply with police requests in routine matters.

Public acceptance of the police role has been achieved by the recognition that the police must have the right to use force in certain circumstances if they are to be effective. It has also been widely recognised that public support for the police is directly related to the manner in which lawful force is applied or the manner in which the right to use force is abused. The police historian, Charles Reith, saw this as a principle in itself which was stated thus, 'To recognise always that the extent to which the co-operation of the public can be secured diminishes, proportionately, the necessity of the use of physical force and compulsion for achieving police objectives.'[9]

The coercive aspect of police powers was summarised by the Royal Commission on Criminal Procedure as follows:

> In many cases they should and will achieve their objectives with the consent (which should be free and genuine) of the person concerned. But they need to be provided with powers to enable them to carry out such activities lawfully and, in the last resort, with application of reasonable force; such powers may be termed coercive. The use of this term does not imply that the police commonly rely on force or the threat of force in the performance of their duties.[10]

The exercise of these coercive powers necessarily involves an intrusion upon the individual, his property or a deprivation of his liberty and the Royal Commission emphasised that they should not be used against a person unless that person was known to have committed or was suspected on reasonable grounds of having committed a specific crime. In addition the exercise of coercive powers must be capable of being justified as necessary in all the circumstances and be capable of immediate challenge and subsequent review.[11]

This was a restatement of principle which incorporated necessity, justification and accountability but the Commission found that there was difficulty in applying this principle to all situations in which the police were required to act and in which some coercive power was required. The minimum use of force implies that the force used should be only sufficient to achieve the purpose required and while the exercise of coercive powers could be justified where persons had committed or were reasonably suspected of committing crime, an extension of these powers to situations where a person was not necessarily suspected of a specific crime or in situations which would normally be unacceptable to the public required very careful assessment.

The Commission adopted the criteria of effectiveness and seriousness and concluded that circumstances might arise requiring the application of a power which of its nature would be unacceptable in the normal run of cases; intimate personal searches, the taking of certain body samples, prolonged detention or detention without allowing access to legal advice. In assessing whether such powers should be available and the special safeguards to be applied to them, they concluded that account must be taken of the effectiveness of the power and of the importance that society placed in bringing those suspected of it to trial. The seriousness of the offence was, accordingly, a critical consideration.[12]

The difficulties in applying a criterion of seriousness were acknowledged. How would it be possible to determine the importance which the public attach to a particular offence? The maximum penalty is a guide but is too imprecise and the Commission pointed out that it would encompass both too much and too little. In recognising that the police must have the necessary investigative powers to deal with very serious crime, the Commission stressed that there must be some way of limiting the availability and controlling the exercise of those powers and this would include specifying the offences or type of offences to which they were to be applied.[13]

The Commission offered a category of 'grave offences'[14] where coercive powers should be available but they acknowledged, 'Parliament will wish most carefully to scrutinise the offences that would warrant the application of the enhanced powers to them since here the balance between the liberty of the citizen and the interests of society is at its most delicate.'[15]

The recommendations made by the Commission sought to achieve this fine balance and this approach is illustrated by their consideration of physical force to obtain body samples.

> There is a case in some circumstances for the police to be able to take samples from a suspect or to submit him to medical examination without his consent. . . . Physical compulsion is unlikely to be effective, because it is difficult to take such body samples by force from a person who is determined to resist, and the use of such force is inherently objectionable.[16]

Nevertheless, although the Commission felt that the obtaining of intimate body fluids such as blood or semen was objectionable, they concluded that less intimate body samples such as hair, scrapings from finger nails or even saliva could be obtained by compulsion.[17] The Royal Commission were endeavouring to strike a balance between the interests of the public and the interests of an accused person. They adopted the view that the interests of society would be outweighed by the liberty of the citizen in those cases where intimate body samples were required.

The principle of minimum force is relevant to the exercise of coercive powers and in determining the minimum force necessary in the investigative process, regard must be had to the objective to be achieved. There is clearly a duty on the police to obtain the best evidence whether for or against the accused but it seems that the Royal Commission properly concluded that certain intimate searches were by their nature an infringement of basic rights. Criticism of subsequent proposals introduced in a Bill before Parliament prompted a further review and there was a strong body of opinion that the intimate body searches for investigative purposes without the consent of an accused should not be allowed.

The use of coercive powers by the police requires careful monitoring so as to eliminate, as far as possible, indiscriminate or arbitrary use. Similarly, there should be adequate safeguards which provide for an immediate review and investigation of police conduct when allegations of abuse are made. The Royal Commission's attempt to rationalise police coercive powers came at a time when there had been considerable public disquiet over allegations of police brutality and street incidents in which it had been alleged that the police had adopted hard or aggressive methods.

Such allegations were made after the Brixton disorders and 'hard policing', involving vigorous efforts to control street crime, was criticised by Lord Scarman in his report.[18] In the context of Brixton, hard policing was identified with the use of the Special Patrol Group on the streets, the arrest of suspected persons loitering in public and the exercise of the coercive power of stop and search.[19] Nobody doubted the need for the police to take effective measures to control serious crime but their efforts were viewed against a background of mistrust, racial prejudice and alleged brutality. Allegations of harassment were numerous and the few incidents of identified police abuse fuelled rumours among the local community. As was put in evidence before Lord Scarman, 'We do not object to what they (the police) do so much as to the way they do it.'[20]

The conclusions reached by Lord Scarman are discussed elsewhere, but in discussing the principle of minimum force it is sufficient to recognise that his conclusions were based on the premise that the objectives of the police to control serious street crime could have been achieved in other ways. On that basis, the force implicit in coercive powers was unjustified and unreasonable.

On the other hand, it was argued that criminals must be sought out, pursued and arrested irrespective of the effect of the methods employed upon innocent people. The objection was that the balance was weighted too heavily in these circumstances against the interest and freedom of the individual. The police took the view that it was weighted too heavily against the interest of the public at large who expected a positive police response to control the high level of street crime.

Such is the dilemma facing the police in a democracy. Whenever the 'public interest' or 'society' is referred to it is normally related to the majority view yet I have already indicated how difficult it is to determine public opinion especially in a multi-racial or plural society.[21] The value of democracy is that it enables the minority view to be heard. Criticism of the majority view is encouraged since this allows reasoned debate on particular issues. If this criticism is stifled or the minority feel that their views are repeatedly ignored, history has shown that frustration spills over into disorder and the police are then required to suppress unlawful violence and rioting by the use of force.

By adopting the principle of minimum force, the police have succeeded in maintaining law and order in a manner which has attracted public support and which has dispelled any fear or suggestion that they are acting on behalf of central government to stifle opposition. This success has not been achieved easily and the importance of the police role in our society is still not widely recognised or understood. They derive their power and authority from the people and this would be forfeited immediately if the police were ever to be used to restrain or suppress the will of the people. The principle of minimum force, together with other established police principles, ensure that the police could never be used in this way.

Nevertheless, it is politically attractive to criticise police action in controlling serious disorder. The lawful use of force by the police is the visible sign of authority and an obvious target for those who would urge for a change in the nature of our society. What is often ignored is the contribution which the police have made to civilised society in maintaining the rule of law by the use of minimum force. It has been emphasised by one historian that 'the degree of physical force which they are obliged to exercise in the course of their daily duties is infinitesimal compared with the immense and highly effective 'preventive' force of their presence and prestige'.[22]

This puts the coercive element of the police function into its proper perspective but since that statement was made, events have occurred which threaten to change the manner in which the police respond to disorder. It is clear from the events at Brixton and elsewhere which involved street disorders on a large scale that the principle of minimum force proved difficult to sustain. At Brixton, in particular, the police were compelled to adopt a defensive role in the face of overwhelming odds. The courage, bravery and resilience shown by many officers against a battery of petrol bombs, missiles and general hostility is now part of police history and, as the story unfolded on television screens across the country, the restraint of the police in the face of extreme provocation earned the respect and admiration of the public who witnessed an open threat to civilised society.

In a situation where the rioters seem intent on using maximum force, a principle of minimum force seems inappropriate but if the police objective is to disperse the rioters and restore order, and they are obliged to achieve it by using such force as is necessary, then that force may have to be considerable. Water hoses were used at Brixton and the police at Toxteth were obliged to use CS gas in order to gain control of desperate situations. In large scale riots, it is also difficult for individual officers to assess the whole situation and their actions must be judged on what they themselves see the situation to be at the time. Uppermost in their minds must be their duty to restore order as soon as possible.

At Brixton, it was inevitable that there should be criticism of the police and allegations were made of brutality and aggressive behaviour. It was alleged that they used unlawful weapons and that they used police dogs, shields and truncheons improperly; it was also alleged that they used unnecessary force and adopted undesirable tactics in order to suppress the disorders. It was suggested that it was only the presence of a militant police force on the streets which kept the rioters rioting and prevented them from dispersing.[23]

These allegations suggested collectively that the police had used more force than necessary in dealing with the disorders. Lord Scarman found that there was some substance in the allegations and he was particularly concerned over allegations that some police officers had used unlawful weapons during the disorders. In a service which has traditionally relied on minimum force, such allegations were of particular significance. In addition, the unfortunate death of a man during street disorders at Southall in 1979 had raised serious questions as to how far some officers had armed themselves with unauthorised weapons in order to combat street disorders. The allegations at Brixton, therefore, merely added fuel to an already sensitive issue.

Lord Scarman's enquiry found that some officers had reacted to the rioters during the disturbances by picking up bricks and other missiles and throwing them back at the crowd.[24] This was understandable in the circumstances but could not be excused in law unless done in self-defence. Other more serious allegations were that some officers were in possession of offensive weapons.[25] Such allegations call into question the whole principle of minimum force and the balance which has to be achieved when controlling public disorder. It was stressed that it was essential that police officers engaged in public order duties should only possess and be known to possess authorised items of equipment.

On the other hand, chief officers and police authorities had a responsibility to ensure that the equipment available to the police was adequate for them to be able to fulfil their task.[26]

This represents the clear limits of the principle in that in the ultimate analysis, street disorder must be controlled and, in order to achieve that objective, the police are empowered to use such force as may be necessary. The response of the police is therefore dictated by the degree of violence and resistance which they meet. The circumstances at Brixton were unprecedented and the police responded instinctively with the limited means at their disposal.

It is not difficult to understand the real apprehension felt by many officers at the height of the rioting. They were ill-equipped and unprepared to withstand the full weight of attack from petrol bombs and other missiles and they were obliged to adopt defensive tactics to try to contain the situation. It would have been of little comfort to them to be reminded that they should remain calm and restrained in the face of extreme provocation and it would not be surprising if some officers had not armed themselves with unauthorised items if they believed they might ultimately need them in order to defend themselves.

The traditional nature of British policing has always been distinguished from other countries by the capacity to suppress disorder by concentrating large numbers of unarmed officers in order to disperse the crowd. The effectiveness of this method has also relied on the reluctance of the public to challenge the rule of law by violent means whilst the weakness of the method is that it is vulnerable to aggressive tactics such as missile throwing. The latter tactic had been widely publicised on television during disorders in Northern Ireland and it was soon taken up by the 'apprentices of violence' masquerading under the banner of football supporters.

Several incidents had occurred in connection with soccer hooliganism and other disorders which had prompted the police to train themselves in the use of protective shields. Whilst these had proved effective as a defensive measure, they tended to frustrate the police involved from turning a defensive situation into an offensive one in which the missile throwers could be arrested or dispersed.

This point was made by Lord Scarman when he referred to the possible danger that protective shields carried by police officers could serve to attract missiles from a crowd. The result was that

officers became targets for the crowd to aim at and the police had
to adopt a largely defensive posture. He thought there was scope
for the police to adopt a more positive interventionist role in
quelling disorder and that they should develop techniques to meet
the threat of the petrol bomb.[27]

The Home Secretary had witnessed the effects of inadequate
protection when visiting injured police officers in hospital after
the disturbances. He commented that there was no such thing as
complete protection against possible injury but that those who
faced inevitable risks as part of their duty to the community were
entitled to the best protection available. He stressed that policing
should be positive and that police officers should not have to stand
immobile while missiles were thrown at them.[28]

Steps were immediately taken to issue fire-proof clothing and
shields; positive tactics were introduced into public order training
and the Home Secretary gave notice that it was his intention to
make water cannon, CS gas and plastic bullets available in
reserve to police forces. Officers appearing in protective helmets,
visors and fireproof suits, together with new style shields, were
barely recognisable as the traditional British police officer and
were immediately compared with their continental colleagues
across the English Channel.

British policing had reached the crossroads and there were
many who viewed this fundamental change of policy with
concern. CS gas had already proved a doubtful method of crowd
dispersal in Northern Ireland for its effective use depended on a
variety of factors such as wind condition and its effect on people in
a particular area could be indiscriminate. Similarly, the plastic
bullet had the potential to cause very serious injuries and, if not
used under strictly controlled conditions, innocent bystanders
could be injured. Unless it was used againt a particular individual
who was offering a serious threat such as a petrol bomb or other
missile, it might be difficult to justify its use. Many thought its
use would be justified in certain situations involving a serious riot
and, if proper warnings of its intended use were given, there
should not be any innocent bystanders.

Lord Scarman's recommendations on the use of such offensive
measures summed up the dilemma facing the police service which
traditionally had relied on the principle of minimum force. He
said that it would be tragic if attempts to bring the police and the
public closer together were to be accompanied by changes in the

manner of policing disorder which served only to distance the police further from the public. He welcomed the fact that most chief officers had agreed on the need to preserve the traditional appearance and role of the police officer in dealing with public order.[29]

In recognising the importance and the necessity of the Home Secretary's decision to make water cannon, CS gas and plastic bullets available to police forces, he recommended that they should only be used in a 'grave emergency' and only on the authority of the chief officer himself. In relating their use to the objective to be achieved, he defined a 'grave emergency' as 'circumstances in which there is a real apprehension of loss of life'.[30] He was endorsing the principle of minimum force since only a real fear of loss of life could justify the use.

It should not be overlooked that there was no suggestion that the British police were intending to adopt or create an independent force to quell disorders and riots. Other countries had long relied on a 'third force' based on para-military lines, such as the Gendarmerie Nationale of France, the Carabinieri of Italy or the National Guard in the United States. Such forces operate independently of the civilian police force and have the capacity and capability of restoring order by the use of force. Their use is usually confined to those situations where traditional methods are incapable of restoring order and, while their use is strictly regulated, it is difficult to divorce them from being associated with central government.

In the aftermath of Brixton, it would have been tempting for the British police to have opted for a similar specialist group in order that the image of the traditional police officer was not de-valued. What emerged was an enhanced system of mutual aid between forces whereby highly-trained officers, fully protected and better equipped, could respond at short notice to spontaneous disorders and deal effectively with them. Equally important was the insistence that ordinary police officers would be mobilised to fulfil this task and this would eliminate the development of specialist groups who would become remote from ordinary contact with the public.

This preserved the traditional approach to disorder whereby the initial response would be a persuasive one followed by a more firm and forceful approach when there were clear indications that the objective of quelling the disorder was not being achieved. As a last resort, the police had the capacity to adopt a positive approach to a threatening situation by the use of water cannon or other extreme measures.

There were many who viewed this fundamental change in the police role with some misgiving but the events at Brixton, Toxteth and elsewhere had represented a fundamental change in the capacity of certain elements in society to create disorder and threaten the rule of law itself.

Reassurances by the Home Secretary to the House of Commons with regard to the use of CS gas and plastic bullets (baton rounds) emphasised that they would only be used as a last resort when conventional methods of policing had been tried and failed, or must by the nature of the circumstances be unlikely to succeed. The decision for their use would be that of the chief officer of police who alone would judge the necessity. In qualifying those circumstances in which he thought it would be necessary, the Home Secretary went beyond Lord Scarman's 'grave emergency' involving a real apprehension of loss of life and included the mere risk of loss of life, serious injury or widespread destruction of property.

Despite this apparent extension of what could amount to the last resort, in practice it will be for the chief officer of police to decide in the light of the prevailing circumstances. The police have a clear and absolute duty to maintain law and order and reliance is now placed on adequate training, more positive tactics and better protective clothing. It should hopefully prove unnecessary to use the more offensive types of equipment which would represent a departure from the traditional approach to public order but it must be recognised that the nature and degree of public disorder have already changed and the police must have the capacity to control violent riots. It was thought to be essential that reserve facilities should be available as a last resort otherwise the only option would be to call in the army to assist.

Whether society as a whole has learned any lessons from the disorders of 1981 remains to be seen. It has been said that a society gets the police it deserves and one police historian, speaking some ten years before the Brixton disorders, made the prophetic comment that:

There are changes occurring now in the police system and there are changes taking place in society. The conjunction of these two is in danger of threatening the mildness of the system and indeed the whole ethos of our policing. I think they are threatening in a way that could lead to something not very far short of a breakdown in our traditional system, unless we recognise the nature of the system and adjust our police and, less hopefully, our society.[31]

By training the ordinary police officer to deal with spontaneous disorder, the British police have survived a crisis of confidence by clinging steadfastly to the principle of minimum force. The ordinary officer, already trained to think and act as an individual, has had to learn to act collectively to combat street disorders. By providing him with proper protection and equipment, he now has the confidence to deal effectively with riot situations.

The final comment on the use of force to contain disorder can be left to the Home Secretary who, commenting on the government's response to serious disorder, said, 'The police must be able to respond to changed circumstances, but do not let us over-react either way. We must adhere firmly to the principle of minimum force and we must concentrate on deploying that minimum force with maximum effectiveness.'[32]

A discussion on the principle of minimum force would not be complete without reference to the ultimate force available to the British police, namely, firearms. For some years, the police have always had a limited capacity to neutralise an armed threat to the public or themselves but the escalation of terrorist offences, armed sieges and hostage situations, together with a general escalation in the use of firearms by criminals, dictated that the police should re-assess their capability to respond. The last decade has seen the emergence of specialised tactical firearms units which have been deployed in serious operational incidents where there has been a clear armed threat to life.

The various incidents in which the police have been obliged to use the firearms have naturally attracted public concern and it has been necessary to set out clear guidelines for the police in order that the use of firearms can always be justified in the circumstances. When applying the principle of minimum force, it can be concluded that the use can only be justified where there is an armed threat to the life of the police officer or some other person. If the person offering the armed threat is killed the action of the police must be critically examined and thoroughly investigated to ensure that there is sufficient justification to establish that the homicide was lawful.

The use of 'deadly force' by the police has aroused much controversy in the United States where individual police departments have varying policies as to the circumstances in which firearms can properly be used. When the United States followed the British police system in the middle of the nineteenth century, the various police forces established at that time were not armed. It is probable that the violent deaths of police officers in the early years, especially in the larger cities of the east coast with large immigrant populations and social unrest, caused many officers to arm themselves for protection. After the Civil War, it is thought that many urban and frontier police officers retained weapons issued during the war. In any event, by the end of the nineteenth century, it was common practice for police departments to arm their officers with official weapons.

The violent nature of American society is often over-stated yet the high level of violent crimes involving firearms indicates a society which accepts the ever-present threat of violence and the need for the police to be armed accordingly. The following observations must be considered against the historical background of American society, but they do assist an understanding of the principle of minimum force and its application to policing generally.

It has been pointed out by one American commentator that men lived and died violently in the middle and far west of the United States long before the emergence of organised crime and he goes on to suggest that there are many law-abiding Americans who consider violent outbreaks to be an evil but necessary feature of a vigorous race.[33] Modern crime is regarded as the legacy of the frontier spirit where lawlessness prevailed and could only be controlled by the gun. The acceptance of the widespread possession of firearms in accordance with the Constitution is reflected in the acceptance of a well-armed and strong police force to control the worst excesses of this violent heritage. The degree of minimum force necessary to control such a society is obviously going to be greater than in this country but nevertheless there is public concern that the use of such armed force by the police is well regulated and subject to critical review.

Since British police officers are unarmed, the use of firearms against armed criminals can be more easily regulated because policies and guidelines are related to the *issue* of the weapon as well as defining the circumstances in which the firearms can lawfully be used to protect life. The strength of such policies lies in the accuracy of the information which leads to the issue of the weapon and the safeguards which exist in order to monitor the use under close supervision.

The American experience is vastly different since being already armed, the only regulatory element lies in departmental policy and the capacity to implement that policy by training and supervision. The statistics relating to civilians killed by police officers are a matter of wide concern and the estimated figures are thought to average 250–300 a year.[34] The concern is not only regarding the number of persons killed but the legal basis for police action. It is recognised that a police officer is entitled to defend himself but the main point of criticism is the 'fleeing felon' rule which is still operative in many states.

In 1962, the American Law Institute issued a model penal code which limited the police use of deadly force to the defence of life or against suspected felons where there was a substantial risk that the person to be arrested would cause death or serious bodily injury if apprehension was delayed. Up to the beginning of 1981, only eight states had formally adopted this code which was designed to eliminate the fleeing felon rule.

The origins of the rule can be traced to the English common law which had recognised serious crimes as felonies and had provided that such felonies were punishable by death. Since the common law formed the basis of American law, felonies such as murder, robbery, rape, arson, burglary, larceny and escape from lawful custody would all have attracted the death penalty. State penal codes adopted the rule which gave legal authority for the police to shoot at a 'fleeing felon'. Such a rule glossed over the finer points of how the officer was expected to make a quick judgement on whether he reasonably suspected the person running away to be a felon.

With the suspect running away, there could be no basis for suggesting the shooting was done in self-defence or in defence of another's life nor could it be suggested that the officer was preventing a felony. The only primitive justification would have been found in the fact that at the end of the eighteenth century, felonies were punishable by death and it could have been said that the felon took the risk of losing his life when committing the crime in the first place. However, it is difficult to justify the retention of the rule where the death penalty has virtually ceased to exist and the category of felonies has been widened to include less serious offences.

Several test cases have been brought in recent years by civil rights action groups with a view to Courts of Appeal declaring that the 'fleeing felon' rule is unconstitutional by denying the suspect the right to live', one of the fundamental rights set out in the American Constitution.[35] Different Courts of Appeal have failed to agree on the issue and the United States Supreme Court has not yet made a constitutional ruling on the matter. It has been left to individual states to amend their respective penal codes but it is clear that many are reluctant to do so.

Many police departments have now excluded the rule but not without hostility from police officers who considered the rule afforded them considerable protection. Despite the effect on morale, some chief officers have taken positive steps to revise policies and guidelines in order to minimise the risk of innocent people being shot. In the cities where the policy has been confined to the defence of life only, there is evidence that the number of civilian deaths has decreased with no apparent increase in the number of police officers killed on duty.

The constitutional conflict in America arises from the right to bear arms and the right not to be deprived of life or limb. Firm and clear guidelines to police officers and high standards of firearms training are considered essential, not only for the protection of police officers and the public, but also to ensure that civil actions in cases of accidental or careless shootings can be defended. Inadequate or improper firearms training has been held to be a 'lack of reasonable care' in negligence claims.[36]

The training of police officers in the use of firearms seeks to achieve a highly disciplined approach in an armed threat situation, so that an officer will know instinctively that there are some situations where he must not discharge his weapon even though a threat to life exists. The decision to shoot must be a personal one and an officer has to rely on justification in law if his actions are called into question. Training also includes psychological factors and simulated stress situations since the unpredictability of an armed threat may be matched by the unpredictability of an officer's response. Nevertheless, training can never really provide a substitute for the reality of experience and the high level of stress on officers who face an armed threat to themselves or others.

The risk of innocent people being shot in this country has always been considered minimal but an incident in London in January 1983 provoked a public outcry when it was found that police officers had opened fire on an innocent man believing him to be an armed escapee from prison. The apparent absence of justification led to the two police officers being charged with attempted murder, and although they were subsequently acquitted, the incident and the verdict caused considerable disquiet.

The Home Secretary was obliged to address the House of Commons and account for the police action. He reiterated the existing rules covering the use of firearms by the police which restricted the use to cases of absolute necessity. A police officer could only resort to firearms as a means of defence if he, or a person he is protecting, is attacked by a person with a firearm or other deadly weapon and he cannot otherwise protect himself or give protection.

The opposition party raised two points of concern which touched on the principle of minimum force. Firstly, that the police must not only be convinced of the absolute necessity to fire but must, wherever possible, warn the target of the intention to open fire. The second point touched on the attitude of the public towards the use of armed force and it was said that to be effective the police needed the support and the confidence of the public, but they would retain neither if they gave the impression that they were acting in an undisciplined fashion or taking the law into their own hands and acting as judge, jury and executioner.[37]

Fresh guidelines were subsequently issued which stressed that firearms should only be used as a last resort and emphasised the individual responsibility of the officer who actually uses the weapon. Public concern was again aroused in April 1983 following reports that the police in Manchester had introduced armed partols to combat a spate of armed robberies in the city. It was necessary to reassure the public that there were no routine or random patrols but that there was a limited armed operation following a 'strong and predictable' threat that criminals might resort to firearms.

The police use of firearms had become a dramatic and sensitive issue for debate but further armed incidents in London and elsewhere, resulting in police officers being killed or wounded provided ample justification for the police to maintain a capability for immediate response by armed officers. *The Times*, whilst supporting the controlled use of firearms by the police, pointed out the dangers on the other side if further cases of mistaken identity occurred and innocent people were shot. It would alienate public goodwill and an increase in the use of firearms by the police also presented further dangers to the public. It was thought it might encourage an urban arms race, with criminals increasingly ready to use as well as brandish guns, to the greater risk of bystanders and those involved.[38]

The use of armed force by the police will always be a controversial issue since it is alien to the traditional role of the police in British society and there is real concern that if violent armed crime continues to increase that armed police officers will be engaged in routine patrols. It is then only a small step away from a general arming of the police which would drive a wedge between them and the public who would not consent to such a radical change. Clear policies and firm guidelines, together with accountability to the law and the courts, are at present sufficient to allay public anxiety but the same policies, guidelines and accountability have proved an insufficient guarantee of public safety in America.

The key to the issue lies in the nature of society. In Britain, the increasing issue of firearms to the police is an indication of the escalation in the use of firearms by criminals and it is vital that the police have the capacity to respond effectively. As with additional equipment for controlling public disorder, the police must be able to deal with any element in society which is minded to use force in the unlawful pursuit of individual or collective objectives. To do otherwise would be a negation of their duty to protect life and maintain order.

It is in the nature of police duty and the enforcement of law that compulsion or force must occasionally be used in order that the police can be effective. Without enforcement, the law is sterile and without effective laws, the result is anarchy. It is seldom realised by those who unjustifiably criticise the use of force by the police that the principle of minimum force exists. Civil liberty action groups rightly draw attention to the occasional lapses in police performance yet fail to emphasise how crucial the police role is to civil liberty itself.

The lawful and regulated use of force by the police is the way in which society is able to preserve the rule of law and the basic freedom of the individual. The principle of minimum force ensures that these liberties are preserved in an acceptable way.

7 The Principle of Prevention

The origin of this principle can be traced to the influential writings of the Fielding brothers and Patrick Colquhoun during the latter half of the eighteenth century.[1] A common thread of their reforming influence was that the objectives of a system of policing should be the prevention and detection of crime, the maintenance of order and the improvement of morals. They were concerned with the whole sphere of justice, the effectiveness of the law and the means of enforcing it.

Prevention of crime was not a new idea. The Anglo-Saxon methods of 'keeping the peace' and the later system of mutual pledging included the notion that crimes could be prevented by the vigilance of one's neighbours or by obedience to higher authority, both terrestrial and celestial. The system of 'watch and ward' proved an effective measure by securing towns during the hours of darkness. The effectiveness of the law, itself, was an important preventive measure and it was the inability of the justice of the peace and the local constable to control increasing crime and disorder which prompted the movement for the reform of the police system.

The emphasis placed by the Fieldings and Colquhoun on prevention is apparent from their respective writings and, while it might have been hoped that obedience to law and the influence of morality would be a strong regulating factor in society, they realised that firm practical measures were also necessary. Henry Fielding's celebrated *Enquiry into the Causes of the Late Increase in Robbers, Etc.* and his *Covent Garden Journal* were both designed to promote public awareness of the causes and dangers of uncontrolled crime and disorder and the ineffectiveness of the law in regulating it.

His declared purpose in writing the *Enquiry* was to '. . . rouse the civil power from its present lethargic state'.[2] His brother,

John, later added his own contribution to the debate and put forward suggestions for the prevention of burglaries and robberies.[3] In echoing his late brother's concern, John Fielding asserted that, 'Unless the dignity of civil power be supported, anarchy must soon take place of authority, and indecency and confusion trample on peace and good order.'[4]

The dangers present in society at the time included the regular disorders in London by rioting mobs, together with uncontrolled lawlessness, drunkenness and immorality. The remedies proposed by the Fieldings were designed to prevent and control general disorder by imposing severe restrictions on drinking, gaming and disorderly houses. This strong moral theme was extended to the eradication of indecent shows, obscene literature and even street singers. The latter were considered undesirable not only because of the obscene songs which idealised the criminal and vice but because the large crowds which gathered gave an opportunity for widespread thieving by pickpockets.

The original approach to preventing crime and disorder was based on severe penalties and strict enforcement. This merely highlighted the ineffectiveness of the existing police system and also the corrupt system of justice based on the local magistrate. To compensate for this ineffectiveness, the Fieldings saw the value in publicising crime and the activities of criminals.

The *Covent Garden Journal* invited members of the public to report robberies and burglaries and to provide descriptions of the suspects. This practice was continued in the *Public Advertiser* and later in the *Quarterly Pursuit of Criminals* and *Weekly or Extraordinary Pursuit*. The public were urged to report all crimes to the Magistrates' office at Bow Street. Details were circulated widely and advice was often given to shopkeepers and others on how to prevent fraud by describing the methods adopted by criminals.

The practice of reporting crime and describing criminals, together with a description of stolen property proved an effective measure and a regular system of circulation throughout London and the rest of the country was established. The success of the scheme led John Fielding to refer to it as his 'favourite preventive machine', but the preventive aspect was largely based on the success in bringing offenders to justice. The scheme also required an efficient system of arresting offenders once they had been identified and the efforts of the Fieldings to establish regular patrols to pursue offenders and prevent their escape are well documented.[5]

The foundations laid by the Fielding brothers are now well recognised and there is little doubt that the seeds of the principle of prevention had been sown before Patrick Colquhoun succeeded in making this principle a feature of his 'new science' of policing.[6] The writings of Colquhoun contain many references to the social and economic problems of the time but his famous *Treatise*[7] represented the first real attempt at analysing the extent of crime in London. The full title of the work shows that its objective was to explain 'The Various Crimes and Misdemeanours Which At Present Are Felt As A Pressure Upon the Community; and Suggesting Remedies for Their Prevention'.

The importance of Colquhoun's work lies in his attempt to look at and identify the causes of crime and the methods by which crimes could be prevented. He saw the police as a restraining influence on 'the facilities by which criminality is nourished and assisted'.[8] Colquhoun had identified the connection between indigence and crime and he emphasised the distinction between indigence and poverty. In an interesting survey of society he concluded that 'Poverty . . . is the lot of man – it is the source of wealth, since without poverty there would be no labour and without labour there could be no riches, no refinement, no comfort . . .'[9] He went on to state that 'Indigence . . . is that condition in society which implies want, misery and distress. It is the state of anyone who is destitute of the means of subsistence and is unable to labour to procure it . . .'[10]

In recommending extensive measures to provide assistance to the 'useful poor', the 'indigent poor', the 'aged and infirm', the 'infant poor' and even to discharged prisoners and prostitutes, Colquhoun sought to prevent crime by preventing indigence.

> . . . [I]t is a state of indigence fostered by idleness, which produces a disposition to moral and criminal offences, and they are so linked together that it will be found impracticable to ameliorate the condition of the poor without taking more effectual measures at the same time for the prevention of criminal offences.[11]

Colquhoun classified indigence as irremediable, remediable and culpable. Culpable indigence included various personality defects such as immoral habits, laziness and 'systematic criminality'. It was to be found among the labouring classes and 'from a state of indigence, wretchedness and despair, the transition is easy to criminal offences'.[12] Whether the causes of crime were due to Fielding's 'social emulation'[13] or to Colquhoun's 'indigent and noxious classes' is largely a matter for social historians. What is undoubtedly clear is that crime and disorder were symptoms of a social disease which was spreading and for which no effective cure had been found.

Colquhoun had painted a gloomy picture of moral degeneration and although he had tended to simplify the complex social and economic structure he was in no doubt that urgent measures were required.

> The evil propensities incident to human nature appear no longer restrained by the force of religion, or the influence of the moral principle. On these barriers powerful attacks have been made, which have hitherto operated as curbs to unruly passions peculiar to vulgar life; they must therefore be strengthened by supports more immediately applicable to the object of preserving peace and good order.[14]

Although the severity of the criminal law should have been an effective preventive measure and deterrent, Colquhoun realised that a system of preventive policing was required which would exercise supervision and restraint over the criminal and working classes with the object of promoting a general moral improvement. He advocated a revision of the criminal law so that it reflected his own moral attitude and would extend to violations against religion and virtue, adultery being included. He recognised that enforcement could be improved by offering greater incentives to informers and that justice could be improved by the appointment of special prosecutors and stipendiary magistrates.

His emphasis on prevention included an organised system of supervision over certain types of premises, certain trades and particular groups. His attack on the sources and causes of 'culpable indigence' was supported by a principle of restraint which he hoped would encourage 'the criminal, the idle and the dissolute members of the community into the paths of innocence and industry'.[15] This system of restraint was thought to be justified on the grounds that the prevention of crime was associated with moral improvement. He considered it justified to eliminate 'the various and increasing evils arising from ill-regulated public houses, so hurtful to the morals of the lower orders of society, and so injurious to themselves and to the individuals composing their families'.[16]

It is an interesting reflection on social history that the regulation and supervision of licensed premises and other establishments by the police remains an important aspect of preventive policing. The licensing laws are often criticised as an unwarranted restriction on leisure and social activity yet the catalogue of daily incidents arising through drunkenness are all too familiar. The menace of the drunken driver, domestic violence involving wife and child abuse, violent assaults, wanton acts of vandalism, late night disorder and football hooliganism are recurring examples of criminal conduct arising from excessive drinking.

From a preventive point of view, it is important that firm action is taken against drunkenness but it is equally important that the public understand the underlying reasons for police action particularly where it is directed towards regulating innocent social conduct such as drinking. The balance of enforcement must be such that it attracts public support and that it is directed towards identified areas of public concern.

Colquhoun also felt there would be every justification to regulate dangerous and suspicious trades, 'the uncontrolled exercise of which by persons of loose conduct is known to contribute in a very high degree to the concealment, and by that means to the encouragement and multiplication, of crimes'.[17] He also singled out particular groups, such as gypsies, whom he felt should be regulated in order to prevent certain crimes. Trustworthy servants should be registered to protect reputable families; prostitutes should be subjected to more restrictive laws and he advocated a system of reformatory detention.

The control of vagrancy was also a matter of concern and he realised that vagrants and beggars should be regulated in order to reduce opportunities for crime. His remedy for idleness was to suggest special 'villages of industry' where vagrants could be detained. An energetic police force was crucial to his plan and it is of interest that from the origins of the 'sus' law, later enacted in the Vagrancy Act of 1824, arose the concept of preventive legislation which enabled the police to arrest before the criminal had actually committed his crime.

Colquhoun was anxious to point out that 'to punish an individual for threatening to commit an offence, not of a criminal nature, and before he actually commits it, is a new principle in jurisprudence recognised in no other civilised country . . .'[18]. He felt that this principle gave it legal validity and that it was not an arbitrary measure. He could not have foreseen or anticipated that the 'sus' law would still be the subject of critical debate some two centuries later culminating in its eventual repeal.[19]

Colquhoun's concept of a preventive police system required an efficient police and he demonstrated what could be achieved in the field of prevention with his scheme of marine police which had such an impact in reducing the level of crime in the vicinity of the Thames.[20] The theme of preventive policing, later supported by distinguished writers such as Bentham and Chadwick, was firmly established by the time Peel set up the Select Committee on the Police of the Metropolis in 1828. Chadwick was invited to give evidence before the Committee and in his memorandum stated, 'To me it appears that the first great object of a Police . . . is to prevent the commission of crime. The second is when crime has been committed, to detect and to bring to conviction the perpetrators of it.'[21]

This statement of principle and function was embodied in the instructions to the new Metropolitan Police which stated that:

It should be understood, at the outset, that the principal object to be attained is the Prevention of Crime. To this great end every effort of the police is to be directed. The security of person and property, the preservation of the public tranquillity and all the other objects of a Police Establishment, will thus be better effected, than by the detection and punishment of the offender, after he has succeeded in committing the crime.

As one police historian has pointed out, this represented a unique concept which was based on the theory that crime and other breaches of the law could be controlled more effectively by benevolent prevention than by repression. It saw prevention as being 'superior in effectiveness not only to repression but also to detection.'[22]

This principle of prevention has rarely been called into question since, although there appears to be some doubt as to whether the prevention of crime remains the primary object of the police. The Willink Commission in 1962, in summarising the duties of the police, gave priority to the duty to maintain law and order and to protect persons and property. Then followed prevention of crime, detection of criminals and prosecution of offenders in that order.[23] They concluded, 'Basically, their task is the maintenance of the Queen's Peace – that is, the preservation of law and order. Without this, there would be anarchy.'[24]

This view was adopted by Lord Scarman in his report on the Brixton disorders.[25] In describing the functions of the police and the principle of 'consent and balance', he reiterated that the primary duty of the police is to maintain the 'Queen's peace'. 'For in a civilised society, normality is a state of public tranquillity. Crime and public disorder are aberrations from 'normality' which it is the duty of the police to endeavour first to prevent and then . . . to correct.'[26] He went on to say that, 'His priorities are clear; the maintenance of public tranquillity comes first.'[27]

In the context of the Brixton disorders, the principle of prevention appears to have become blurred since the prevention of crime and the prevention of disorder overlap and the question of priorities has to some extent become confused. In dealing with the balance between maintaining order and enforcing the law, Lord Scarman saw the solution of the conflict in giving priority to the maintenance of public order and in the common sense exercise of discretion.[28] This is an over-simplification since other conflicts can arise such as that between preventing crime and preventing disorder.

As a matter of principle, both are connected with prevention but Lord Scarman suggests that the prevention of disorder should take priority over the prevention of crime. As a matter of practice, this raises difficult issues for operational police officers who often regard their traditional role as giving priority to the primary object of preventing crime. It was understandable that the high level of street crime in Brixton, particularly the high incidence of robberies (muggings), should attract special police measures to reduce it. The saturation operation mounted by the police was, with hindsight, regarded by Lord Scarman as a serious mistake. Local consultation and a review of the public order implications of the operation would have suggested it was unwise to continue with it.

The prevention of crime was, therefore, a secondary issue if the measures taken by the police carried a risk of local hostility and public disorder, but the police have a duty to prevent crime and the public have a right to insist they should do so. The problem, as stated by Lord Scarman, was how to cope with a rising level of crime – and particularly of street robbery – while retaining the confidence of all sections of the community, especially the ethnic minority groups.[29] Unfortunately, this question remains un-answered and many critics of Lord Scarman's recommendation that there should be positive discrimination in favour of ethnic minority groups ask why they should be regarded as a special section of the community. Is it because of the social and economic deprivation identified by Lord Scarman or is it because of the fact that positive discrimination will reduce the risk of rioting in the streets?

Social and economic deprivation is not confined to ethnic minority areas and the history of preventive policing reveals that social and economic deprivation has always been a breeding ground for crime. The solution lies in a conscious effort by both central and local government to eradicate deprived areas of the conditions which nurture criminality and give grounds for frustration and organised grievances. It should not be overlooked that deprivation through unemployment and other social factors still persist in some areas. Positive discrimination is required to eliminate deprivation and inequality wherever they manifest themselves and it should not be confined to ethnic minority areas.

A propensity towards violent protest and rioting among a particular group or groups in society appears to be a doubtful criterion on which to base the allocation of resources to assist social reform. It should be dictated by need and need is not determined by the vociferous element in society. A policy of positive discrimination has the appearance of responding to an overt threat and where such a policy is seen by police officers to result in a style of policing which favours one group as against another, the principle of equality under the law becomes strained.

In the final analysis, however, governments are responsible for the maintenance of order. In its purest form, social equality must be regarded as a strong preventive measure against crime and disorder but idealistic theories are no protection against the practical reality of crime and disorder and the difficulties facing the police in trying to prevent them. The police are not concerned with political aspects of social and economic deprivation but they are required to deal with the worst manifestations of deprivation and it is right to recognise that in applying the principle of prevention to the police role there are other fields of preventive action by local and central government which can assist in producing a better social climate in which the police can operate.

A further conflict arising from Lord Scarman's conclusions lies between enforcing the law and preventing disorder. He maintained that priority must be given to the maintenance of public order but what if enforcement of the law involves not crime in the narrow sense, but the enforcement of public order legislation? There are several statutory preventive measures which are aimed at controlling conduct which is intended or likely to cause a breach of the peace.[30] Failure to enforce the law in situations where police action might provoke disorder would lead to the paradox of not preventing a breach of the peace in order to preserve the peace! This could only be justified if the police felt that the enforcement of a comparatively trivial breach or threatened breach of the peace would be likely to provoke a far more serious breach of the peace.

This seems to be straining the principle of prevention too far since it is expecting a fine degree of judgement on the part of a police officer who has to make a spontaneous decision to act. The public would not expect him to ignore an obvious case of disorder on the basis that in his judgement it might provoke a situation he would be unable to cope with. The difficulty with disorder is that police action is often limited to those incidents which they themselves witness and they invariably have a wide discretion as to the way in which they are dealt with.

Occasionally a difficult situation arises that can be satisfactorily handled by tact and a sense of humour rather than by arrest. Much will depend on the attitude, condition and conduct of the others involved, no less than the officer's own attitude, approach and conduct. Uppermost in the officer's mind will be the duty placed on him to prevent disorder and in a hostile situation, it is really asking too much to expect the officer to weigh up the possible consequences and ignore an overt, and often public, attempt to undermine his authority.

The Brixton riots in 1981 provide a good example of the difficulties involved. Serious rioting was sparked off by the arrest of a man for obstructing the police and it was said that this was nothing unusual on the streets of Brixton – two plain clothes officers questioning a suspect, a hostile crowd gathering and complaining of police harassment, an arrest, and a final violent protest as the police sought to remove the arrested man. Usually, however, such an incident would have ended there: the protesting crowd would, after a little while, have dispersed and normality would have returned.[31] The two officers involved in the arrest were criticised for their lack of discretion and judgment in a tense situation but the inference was that they should not only have weighed up the *probable* consequences, based on their experience of the usual, but also the *improbable* consequences which were the unusually serious incidents of rioting which followed.

Although the police were criticised at Brixton for, on the one hand, over-reaction to the disorders and, on the other, delay and lack of vigour in handling the disorders, the circumstances of the rioting provided a good illustration of the varying and conflicting aspects of the principle of prevention. From the police point of view, it provided a new approach in that the prevention of crime was seen as a secondary issue to the prevention of disorder and rioting. Furthermore, it exposed the causes of disorder and the need for collective action to prevent it.

Preventive action by police and public can be extended to the field of consultation and, following the disorders at Brixton and Lord Scarman's criticisms, the police were prompt to examine ways of extending the existing informal and formal consultation with the communities they serve. Local consultation had always been a feature of policing but had rarely been recognised as a preventive function. Consultation properly belongs to a discussion on accountability[32] but it can be an important first step in identifying those problems and conditions which might influence crime or provoke disorder. The police, in their preventive role, are also in a position to recognise tension in a community and consultation can often identify the root causes of unrest and frustration.

Policing policies are now adjusted to accommodate early recognition of social unrest in order that they can be evaluated and acted upon with other agencies. Where tension exists and manifests itself in open hostility towards the police, it is essential that the local leaders of the community are consulted and kept informed of developments. This collective approach will invariably reduce the risk of escalation. It is an example of preventive action which will command public support for subsequent police action and frustrate those elements who would try to exploit the situation for their own purposes.

The principle of prevention can be extended to other situations which have a potential for disorder. They are easier to regulate because they are usually foreseeable and preventive measures can be taken to avoid confrontations between rival sections of the community. Marches and processions can be controlled by preliminary meetings with the organisers when the route, timing and other ground rules can be agreed.

The police, in order to prevent clashes with rival factions, can usually assess the potential for disorder beforehand and additional marches by opposition groups will be strictly controlled to prevent them from converging on the main procession. In a democracy which values the freedom of speech and the right to protest, it is the function of the police to remain impartial and preserve this right no matter how controversial or extreme the views are.

Occasionally it can arise that the potential for disorder is so great that a procession may be banned and chief officers of police can exercise statutory powers to impose conditions such as the route and timing.[33] The limitations on this power to impose conditions was considered by Lord Scarman who commented that it would not be lawful for him to impose conditions the practical effect of which would be to ban the march or procession. 'The power is to impose conditions, not to prohibit processions'.[34]

Where the imposition of conditions would not prevent 'serious public disorder', a chief officer of police can apply to the district council for an order banning any class of public procession for a period of up to three months and this requires the consent of the Home Secretary.[35] Such a decision is not taken lightly since any ban represents a serious curtailment of liberties. A ban can only be justified where it is necessary, in the professional judgement of the chief officer, in order to prevent serious disorder. Regard must be had for the silent majority who themselves have rights and freedoms to preserve.

The banning of processions remains a sensitive issue but the principle of prevention is equally valid in relation to disorder as it is in relation to crime. The preventive function of the police in connection with public order was reviewed in 1980[36] and suggestions for reform included a requirement of advance notice of a procession and less stringent tests for imposing conditions or banning a procession.

Lord Scarman recognised the political and constitutional sensitivity in banning specified processions but recommended that the suggestions for reform be implemented as an amendment to the Public Order Act. There can be no doubt that such legislation would enhance the capacity of the police to deal with potential disorder but it is essential that a balance is maintained between the public interest and the right of the individual to free speech and free association. The passive presence of a large number of police officers is usually sufficient to prevent disorder and ensure that basic liberties are preserved.

The impartiality of the police in dealing with the right to protest is also tested in the area of industrial disputes involving large numbers of pickets and demonstrators. Tension is often high particularly where attitudes have hardened and negotiations have broken down. The principle of prevention is again crucial to the police role and they will invariably rely on a co-operative attitude from the strike leaders and pickets so that lawful picketing can be carried out peacefully. The Code of Practice on Picketing sets out the preventive role of the police and emphasises that they have discretion to take whatever measures may reasonably be considered necessary to ensure that picketing remains peaceful and orderly.[37]

The main cause of violence and disorder is an excessive number of pickets since this facilitates obstruction and intimidation. Pickets often become mingled with demonstrators and well publicised disputes attract the attention of the media and politicians. In such a climate, it is difficult for formal police action not to be interpreted as favouring one side or the other and arrests are only justified in order to prevent an escalation of disorder. Much can be achieved by sensitive handling, tact and good humour since extreme groups will invariably try to provoke an adverse police reaction with all the attendent publicity.

Football hooliganism is another source of recurring disorder which creates much difficulty. Rival supporters, intent on confrontation have, for many years, represented a blight on one of our national games and earned us an unenviable reputation in Europe and elsewhere. The police effort involved in trying to separate rival groups and prevent disorder seems difficult to justify in the name of a commercial activity. The mindless violence which often characterises serious outbreaks of hooliganism could well be prevented if certain football grounds were closed and stronger measures taken against clubs whose supporters show a recurring disregard of the rights of the general public to enjoy the sport.

There is support for the view that every football club should organise its own system of supervision through stewards who should have full powers of ejection in strictly enforcing the ground regulations. The police should not be engaged on duty inside the ground which is private property and a commercial undertaking. This would leave the police free to deal with troublesome elements outside the ground who are ejected and they could concentrate on their primary preventive role on the streets where the public expect them to be. It occasionally happens that an inadequate police presence on the streets in the vicinity of a football ground has been due to an over-concentration of officers inside. The police would still be entitled to enter a football ground to deal with or prevent a breach of the peace.

Police planning of such events has now been developed to a high degree and groups of supporters with a reputation for hooliganism are closely supervised and segregated. There is also plenty of scope for further preventive measures such as limiting the availability of alcohol and removing material and objects that might be used for offensive purposes. Other measures can be taken to improve ground facilities and avoid congestion at turnstiles. There is little doubt that seated supporters are less troublesome than standing ones and the police can often anticipate problems due to early closing of the gates when the ground had reached full capacity.

These practical preventive measures need to be supplemented by the wider application of the preventive principle whereby football clubs arrange for informal schemes to cultivate a closer relationship between troublesome supporters and their local team. Many football clubs now have some form of youth liaison scheme and the police can also play their part by emphasising to young supporters the adverse effect of hooliganism on the success of the club.

This illustration of the various situations and events which often provide the arena for public disorder highlights the difficulties facing the police in applying the principle of prevention. As in other areas of prevention, the police function requires the support of the public and of the law itself. The common law duties to prevent a breach of the peace are well established though not fully defined and the expression 'breach of the peace' is now included in several statutory preventive measures.[38] However, the police are still obliged to deal with some street disorders by relying on a statute originally passed to deal with the rise of fascism in England before the Second World War. The absence of clear authority for police action in such circumstances means that they occasionally have to strain an existing law which is inappropriate for the purpose. Furthermore, they are sometimes compelled to take preventive action where no precise legal authority exists.

Such practical measures are usually required to combat hooliganism and football supporters are often searched indiscriminately for offensive weapons where no reasonable suspicion exists. Recurring incidents of hooliganism at seaside resorts during public holidays have led to the practice of items such as belts and boot-laces being retained by the police as a preventive measure. Even existing statutory measures to prevent crime, especially those relating to the searching of persons and vehicles before arrest, have caused uncertainty in their application.[39]

The Royal Commission on Criminal Procedure commented on 'the need to place on a rational basis and bring into line with modern conditions those procedures and practices, some of which date at least from the last century and in which anomalies are apparent. There is a consensus in favour of codification and rationalisation of the provisions. It is argued further that the resulting clarification, if it could be achieved, would assist the police in preventing and detecting crime, because it would remove uncertainty both for them and the citizen.'[40]

It was understandable that the police should seek increased powers to stop and search persons since they, themselves, recognised that they were forced on occasions to act outside the strict limitations of the law or to rely on general public ignorance of their powers.

In dealing with the powers of the police to stop and search, the Royal Commission commented that 'The police have a duty to protect members of the public from violent attacks. If there is imprecision in the definition of the offence, the remedy for the difficulty . . . lies in removing that imprecision rather than in refusing the police the power to search.'[41] In advocating a general power to stop and search, the Royal Commission sought to distinguish between the use of powers to stop and search in detecting criminal offences and the use of a power to stop as a means of controlling potential threats to public order.[42]

The powers to prevent public disorder were outside the terms of reference of the Royal Commission but they received careful examination by Lord Scarman after the Brixton disorders. He had received a proposal put forward by the Commissioner of the Metropolitan Police to create a new offence of failing to disperse after a public warning. It represented an attempt to revive the old principle embodied in the Riot Act of 1714[43] which had made it an offence to fail to disperse after a public warning by a magistrate. Lord Scarman was not attracted to the proposal and felt the existing law was adequate.

He was not in favour of an offence which was based on a failure to disperse after warning but preferred the principle that there should be positive acts of criminal behaviour by the accused. He also doubted the effectiveness of a public warning given in 'the din of turmoil'.[44] This offers an interesting comparison with Colquhoun's new principle in jurisprudence that persons should be punished for threatening to commit offences.[45] From a preventive point of view, it is clearly preferable to act in some cases before the substantive offence has been committed.

This is the basis for many of the statutory preventive measures under the Public Order Act but there are difficulties associated with such preventive measures as it could be argued they infringe basic liberties. The police are provided with a power of arrest in the preparatory stages of an offence and the evidence involved in such cases is often disputed and the police are criticised for acting prematurely or arbitrarily. The notorious 'sus' law,[46] whereby suspected persons or reputed thieves could be arrested for loitering with intent to commit an arrestable offence was widely criticised by civil rights groups before its eventual repeal in 1981.[47]

A new offence was created of interfering with a vehicle with the intention of stealing it or anything carried on it, or of taking and driving it away without consent. Lord Scarman doubted that the new offence might prove better than the one it replaced and one provision, which states that it is immaterial that it cannot be shown which of the intended offences was being committed by the accused person, was referred to as a juristic anomaly.[48] It was also pointed out that the new offence was much narrower since other street crime as handbag snatching or pickpocketing were no longer included as they were under the former law.

Nevertheless, Lord Scarman saw some advantage in a law which was drafted in terms appropriate for the mischief it was intended to prevent, namely, car theft. He felt this was a step forward from a law which was designed to protect Cobbett[49] and his contemporaries as they moved in their rural rides around the countryside of England in the aftermath of the Napoleonic wars![50] It can be anticipated that there will still be criticism of any law which seeks to control preparatory acts before an offence has been committed but it cannot be challenged on principle if prevention is the objective.

Effective law enforcement and firm action by the courts can also contribute much in the prevention of crime and disorder by deterring those who are minded to engage in such activities. The original preventive role of the police was to patrol the streets so that their mere presence acted as a deterrent. A strong police presence can obviously do much to control crime and disorder but it is important to recognise the limitations of this preventive role particularly in regard to crime.

Firstly, it can be argued that such measures are not wholly effective. As Lord Scarman pointed out, he doubted the efficacy of the street saturation operation in Brixton since it tended to drive criminals elsewhere. In the long term, he thought that a style of policing which secured public approval and respect would be more effective.[51] There is much force in this view but the public expectations of the police role in preventing crime must be fulfilled if the police are to secure public approval and respect.

The second point to bear in mind is that the preventive role of the officer in the street can only be effective against those crimes which occur on or in the vicinity of streets or public places. These can be referred to loosely as 'street crime' and include such offences as robbery, burglary, theft of and from vehicles, other miscellaneous thefts and assaults arising from public order incidents. Such crimes can clearly be prevented to a degree but there remains a wide range of crimes which occur in private such as serious assaults, sexual offences, thefts from shops and premises and many involving fraud and dishonesty, including deception. These crimes, committed away from the public arena, cannot be prevented by patrolling officers but crime statistics, which are used as a yardstick for measuring police efficiency, fail to distinguish between 'public' and 'private' crimes.

When analysing crime statistics, it is apparent that the capacity of the police to detect crime is a limited one. Some recorded crimes, such as handling stolen goods and 'shoplifting' are, by their nature, invariably detected. Since the majority of assaults involve an assailant who is known to the victim, many of these crimes are also detected more readily. If, however, those offences I have referred to as 'street crimes' are considered separately, the ineffectiveness of the police in detecting them is apparent. In order to combat street crime, special measures are often employed such as the use of special plain-clothes officers and this was one of the methods used at Brixton. It can be criticised as placing too great an emphasis on detection rather than prevention. The one reliable measure of efficiency in relation to the prevention of street crime must be a reduction in the number of street crimes reported to the police. We should be reminded of Mayne's statement that the primary object of an efficient police is the prevention of crime and that to these ends all the efforts of the police should be directed. He concluded that the *absence of crime* would alone prove whether the objects for which the Police were appointed had been attained.

The principle of prevention is now recognised as embodying all the preventive functions of the various social agencies and the criminal justice system. The police continue in the dominant role but the general public also have a responsibility to assist in any way possible. Thus an important aspect of the preventive role of the police is to cultivate the public interest in crime particularly within their own locality. It has long been the practice in many urban areas of the United States for small groups within a community to form an effective preventive force which has attracted such titles as 'neighbourhood watch'. The schemes are intended to increase public awareness of crime and to cultivate the public to report all suspicious or unusual incidents in their locality.

The nature of the scheme can vary and it can be adapted to particular locations such as high-rise blocks. It can represent collective policing by the police and public at its best and great emphasis is placed on publicising the scheme in the area. In one scheme in Scarsdale, New York, the employees of the local post office and taxi firms, together with local authority departments, were encouraged to report crime and suspicious incidents. In many cases, use was made of the radio communication systems in the vehicles. The whole effort by the local community was controlled by the police who ran a series of educational and training programmes so that the public could appreciate their role in crime prevention.

The scheme in Scarsdale was extended to citizen band radio operators who were recruited into the Scarsdale Communications Assistance Network (SCAN) and were able to report emergencies and other incidents immediately to the police. The aim was to involve all the community and business groups, civic groups, schoolchildren and ordinary citizens in the scheme and safety and crime prevention advice was widely publicised. A further project called 'Identifax' encouraged citizens to mark valuables and other property with a special coded identification number. The public were constantly reminded of their duty to assist the community in reducing crime by awareness and prevention.

After a given period, the effect of the scheme was analysed and it is claimed that burglaries had been reduced by 25 per cent while reports from the public in relation to suspicious persons and vehicles had doubled. The local chief of police advised the public that they should not take the law into their own hands but should take an active interest in their community by being alert to the unusual or out-of-place activity.'

Neighbourhood Watch schemes have now been developed by the Metropolitan Police and it is clear that there is considerable scope for similar schemes to be adopted throughout the country. The effectiveness of such schemes, however, must be measured against a realistic expectation of deterring the criminal. I have already stressed the fact that the preventive role of the police can only be effective against street crime, that is, those offences which can be seen. It has also been suggested that preventive measures in one area may simply transfer the problem elsewhere.

The modern approach to crime prevention provides an interesting contrast to the original philosophy underlying the principle of prevention. The common link is the attempt to reduce the opportunity for committing crime. Originally, this was best achieved by the physical presence of patrolling police officers. Crime prevention is now concerned with making crime more difficult. The emergence of security organisations to transfer high value loads or to provide preventive patrols for private industrial premises are indications of a growth industry. The widespread use of alarms and additional security for vulnerable premises have become necessary features of modern society.

Nevertheless, it is important to bear in mind the American experience where crime preventive measures have had a drastic effect on the ordinary person. A law has been introduced making it an offence to leave the ignition key in a vehicle; another law requires the installing of lights outside multiple dwellings. It has been pointed out that society lives and responds in order not to become a victim of crime. This has caused a reverse enforcement against the potential victim of crime and people have had their freedom reduced. In addition it has spread the fear of crime.

It is important, therefore, to keep the problem of crime and its prevention in perspective. There is much that can be done by a collective approach by the police and the public. It is preferable that measures such as neighbourhood schemes should be adopted which involve no change in the nature of society and which have no significant effect on day to day life. The principle of prevention was never intended to result in a situation, as in some urban areas of America, where the honest majority has to suffer for the criminal minority.

There has also been a recent commentary on the collective approach by police and public to the prevention of crime which suggests that a new approach is required. It has been advocated that a newer philosophy of policing is required in which policing is not only seen as a matter of controlling the bad but also includes activating the good. It is said:

> This idea represents the point where modern preventive policing tactics part company with the traditional or Peel model. Peel's preventive police were created to control the criminal classes, the mob and the battalions of London's lower orders. It follows in a modern society . . . where most people are potential criminals or victims, that newer preventive policing methods are desirable.[52]

This statement can be challenged on two grounds. Firstly, not many people would regard themselves as potential criminals since crime is identified with the more serious breaches of the criminal law such as murder, robbery, rape, burglary, theft, etc. However, there is no distinction in law between crime in the narrow sense and the volume of regulatory offences which relate to road traffic, betting, gaming and licensing, public health, etc. All breaches of the law which are characterised by the infliction of punishment or penalty by the state are termed 'criminal' and the confusion between the more serious crimes and the wide range of minor offences is perpetuated by the anomaly that a motorist may be fined more for careless driving than a criminal is fined for theft.

Such anomalies as this and the failure to distinguish between proper crime and mere regulatory offences has affected the public's attitude towards crime generally and to the police in particular. It has also been suggested that the general lowering of moral standards and a reluctance to condemn conduct which is manifestly criminal have also had an effect upon the public's reaction to crime. This also has considerable implications in efforts by the police to involve the public in crime prevention schemes. A wider use of the fixed penalty system and separate small courts to deal with regulatory matters would do much to emphasise the true nature of criminal conduct in the eyes of the public and would result in a more favourable attitude to collective action against crime.

The second ground on which this newer philosophy of policing can be challenged is the assumption that newer policing methods are desirable and that modern policing preventive tactics should part company with the traditional Peel model. It is accepted that the original Peel model was intended to deal with the criminal classes and the mob but criminality is ever present and there is little difference between the mob of the early nineteenth century and the rioting mobs at Brixton and Toxteth.

Although society has changed considerably, it is still social and economic deprivation which lies at the root of the problem. Lord Scarman commented that the police did not create social deprivation or racial disadvantage: they are not responsible for the disadvantages of the ethnic minorities and yet their role is critical.

> If their policing is such that it can be seen to be the application to our new society of the traditional principles of British policing, the risk of unrest will diminish and the prospect of approval by all responsible elements in our ethnically diverse society will be the greater.[53]

Policing methods, particularly with regard to prevention, may well change but not at the expense of the traditional model. Tradition is based on principles which are fundamental and which remain valid even if the nature of policing and society changes. This becomes clearer if we examine what is being suggested as a new preventive approach to policing. It is said to operate at three identifiable levels but it is difficult to identify anything new in the suggested approach.

The first level is described as proactive and this refers to those activities which influence people away from criminal activity. It involves co-operation with other agencies in an effort to remove adverse social conditions and to persuade and educate the community to anticipate and recognise criminality so that preventive measures can be taken. The second level is the familiar policing role in preventing crime which includes street patrols and giving advice to businesses and householders. The third level combines the detection of offenders and the corrective influence of the courts, social agencies and penal institutions.[54]

This new philosophy seems to ignore the fact that these three levels have been operating reasonably successfully for some years. It would be a distortion of the policing function to project the police as a vehicle for a collective preventive role which might be seen by many as usurping the function of the existing social agencies. The police do not possess the professional expertise to harness such a wide range of activity. This is not to deny the value of liaison and consultation at all levels and much is achieved in this field at present.

It is right that the police approach to the principle of prevention should be reviewed regularly and new initiatives explored but there is a distinction between function and principle. What is required is a restatement of the principles on which the modern police service is based. The collective responsibility to prevent crime and disorder remains and whether this is dressed up as 'proactive policing' or 'community policing' is largely irrelevant.

Police involvement with the community has been the subject of comment by Her Majesty's Chief Inspector of Constabulary. In acknowledging Lord Scarman's recommendations on styles of policing and consultative committees, he said that it should be recognised that some of these recommendations were already firmly established in police methods and work. He added that the patient efforts, involving considerable resources, which had been made by forces up and down the country to maintain and improve community relations should not be forgotten.[55] He also drew attention to the various schemes which had been introduced and

suggested that the deployment of the officer on the beat could be
even more effective if he was part of a considered scheme to enlist
support from the public.[56]

He also emphasised the traditional approach of deploying large
numbers of officers in ordinary dress to prevent or contain
disruptions and said, ' . . . the integration of public order policing
with policing as a whole is the best practical means of giving effect
in this area, as in others, to the principle that the primary purpose
and aim is prevention'.[57]

8 Independence and Accountability

In his report on the Brixton disorders, Lord Scarman identified two well-known principles of policing a free society. The first was 'consent and balance' and the second, 'independence and accountability'. I have tried in earlier chapters to emphasise the importance of the first of these principles by referring to the various aspects of the police role which are vital in securing and maintaining the consent of the public. Thus a balanced approach to policing, based on ethical standards, the art of discretion and sensitive policing, can do much to secure the consent of the community on whose support the police rely.

The second basic principle concerns the independence of the police and their accountability for their actions. These two concepts of independence and accountability are related since an adequate structure of accountability is necessary if the operational independence of the police is to be preserved. It is in this area that the police are most vulnerable to attack and criticism since any politically inspired measures to undermine the independence of the police inevitably concentrate on a lack of accountability. Any suggestion that the accountability of the police is inadequate is naturally accompanied by a clamour for reform which threatens the independent status of the police.

The importance of preserving the independence of the police and the nature of this independence was referred to by Lord Scarman who commented that:

Neither politicians nor pressure-groups nor anyone else may tell the police what decisions to take or what methods to employ, whether to enforce the law or not in a particular case, or how to investigate a particular offence. The exercise of police judgement has to be as independent as the exercise of professional judgement by a doctor or a lawyer. If it is not, the way is open to manipulation and abuse of the law whether for political or for private ends . . .[1]

The historical basis for the independent status of the police can be found in the origins of the modern police system. The long tradition that local responsibility for law and order was vested in the office of constable also reflected the fact that the powers and duties of the constable were rooted in the common law. The fact that his powers could be said to be original and not delegated supported the view that a constable enjoyed a considerable degree of independence in the exercise of his powers. The constable, therefore, occupied a unique constitutional position but his function became blurred by the influence of the justice of the peace and the later subordination of the constable to the justices.

The justices were officers of the Crown and their prerogative to maintain the 'King's Peace' tended to undermine the principle of local responsibility. The role of the justice was an important one and, in addition to being judicial and administrative, it also involved the control of the constable. This constraint on the constable's common law powers inevitably restricted the scope of his independence but his sworn oath reaffirmed his service to the Sovereign and his fidelity to the law. The oath also emphasised the impartial discharge of his duties 'without favour or affection, malice or ill-will.'

The role of the constable *vis-à-vis* the justice of the peace was reconciled, to some extent, by the fact that they both held office under the Crown. The constable, however, was under the control of the justices and acted under their direction. By the end of the seventeenth century, it was common practice for constables to be sworn in by the justices and this function is still preserved. When the modern police system was created by statute in the early nineteenth century, this subordination was preserved. The retention of the traditional control by the justices was the only way in which the independence and impartiality of the police could be reconciled with a degree of external control which was considered to be politically and constitutionally acceptable.

Once the modern police system had become established, other restrictions on the independence of the police began to emerge. Democratic control was exercised by the Home Secretary over the Metropolitan Police and, in the new borough councils, the appointed watch committees began to assume greater control over the police. In the county areas, the control and influence of the justices survived until 1888 when the newly created county councils established standing joint committees consisting of both justices and local councillors.

It was to be expected that some local democratic control should be imposed on the police in view of the expenditure involved in maintaining a police force. The same principle was applied by central government who appointed an inspectorate to assess the efficiency of police forces. The annual grant from the Exchequer towards the cost of maintaining a police force was sufficient justification and it represented a further element of control over local police forces.

As the role of the justices declined, uncertainty grew as to the precise limits of control by the police authorities. This uncertainty strengthened the position of chief constables who enjoyed a greater degree of independence as a result. This system of local control and central supervision survived the first half of the twentieth century but public disquiet over the efficiency and accountability of the police led to the appointment of a Royal Commission whose report in 1962[2] paved the way for the reforms embodied in the Police Act of 1964.

The Royal Commission addressed their minds to the legal and constitutional position of chief constables and the officers under their control. It is clear from the evidence given to the Commission that the basis for the independent nature of a constable's office arose from the fact that the courts had held that there was no relationship of master and servant as between a police authority and a constable or as between the Crown and the constable. 'In thus denying that he is a servant of either a local or central authority, the courts have been led to assert the independent character of his office.'[3]

The Royal Commission also commented on the difficulty of reconciling the traditional independent status of the constable with his position as a member of a disciplined body subject to the lawful orders of superior officers. The apparent anomaly is explained by the fact that he is often not acting under orders but relies on his own discretion, particularly with regard to suspected offences, arrest of offenders and the decision to report offenders for prosecution.

In matters of this kind, it is clearly in the public interest that a police officer should be answerable only to his superiors in the force and . . . to the courts. His impartiality would be jeopardised, and public confidence in it shaken, if in this field he were to be made the servant of too local a body.[4]

In considering the legal status of a chief constable, the Royal Commission accepted the view that because he holds the office of constable, he therefore enjoys full protection from local control in carrying out his duties of law enforcement and in commanding his force for this purpose.[5] It was difficult to sustain this view in the light of representations from police authorities that they should have some control over a police force which they were required to maintain.

The Commission recognised this conflict which was essentially a rival claim to the former power exercised by the justices over the police. On the one hand, it was asserted that no police authority or anyone else could interfere with the enforcement of the law by the police. The contrary view was that a police authority ought to be entitled to give instructions to a chief constable on such matters as enforcing the law more vigorously or the methods used to deal with political demonstrations.

The Commission, in referring to the position of chief constables said that their claim to a large measure of constitutional independence had been contested by representatives of some police authorities not merely on legal grounds, but on the grounds that a police authority ought, in the public interest, to have some control over the force which it appoints and hence over the chief constable who commands it.[6] It was generally agreed that the quasi-judicial role of chief officers in respect of law enforcement, enquiries, arrest and prosecution should remain independent from external influence or control but the Commission felt that there was general concern over the fact that there was a whole range of other activities for which a chief constable was not accountable.

The fundamental issue concerned the right of chief constables to exercise unfettered discretion over policing policies which involved the public interest. Policies relating to general enforcement, the disposition of his force, the concentration of resources to deal with particular areas of crime, the handling of political demonstrations, processions or industrial disputes, outbreaks of violence, passive resistance to authority and enforcement policies relating to road traffic. The Commission considered a wide range of options which sought to subject a chief constable to a greater degree of supervision and control without compromising his impartiality in enforcing the law in particular cases.

The options ranged from formal reporting to police authorities on matters of policing policies to a consideration of direct control by local authorities or central government. The eventual result of these considerations led to the responsibilities and powers of chief constables, police authorities and the Home Secretary being placed on a statutory footing.[7] The operational independence of chief officers was preserved but measures were introduced to provide greater accountability, particularly in the field of complaints against the police.

Insofar as policies on law enforcement were concerned, the independence of a chief constable was reaffirmed and given judicial approval in 1968.[8] It was held that he had a duty and responsibility to enforce the law and that he was not the servant of anyone except the law itself. The question of independence and accountability continued to be a live issue. The individual constable's independence of action was associated with the exercise of discretion and the impartial discharge of his duties. In a disciplined service, where the individual officer was subject to regulations, instructions and policies, it was natural that the weight of criticism should fall on chief officers who exercised control over their officers.

The Police Act 1964 reflected this relationship between a chief officer and officers under his command by providing that a chief officer of police should be liable in respect of torts committed by constables under his direction and control in the performance or purported performance of their functions in the same way that a master was vicariously liable in respect of torts committed by his servants.[9]

Despite the statutory functions set out in the Police Act 1964, the relationship between a chief officer and his police authority remained obscure. A police authority could call for reports on the policing of an area but its primary function was to maintain an adequate and efficient police force. There was little scope for any erosion of the independent function of the chief officer and accountability was restricted to a statutory duty to keep themselves informed as to the manner in which complaints against the police were investigated.[10]

The absence of local control could be contrasted with an increase in the control exercisable by central government through the Home Secretary. The 1964 legislation provided the Home Secretary with the power to secure compulsory amalgamations, to set up local independent enquiries and to require reports from chief officers on any matter connected with the policing of his area. The effect of these changes was to increase central supervision at the expense of local control and accountability. The effect of amalgamations of police forces was to create in some cases a greater remoteness between the emerging joint authorities and the policing issues in particular localities. Whatever structure of authority is created to maintain an efficient police force, policing remains a local issue and there is some validity in the view that the amalgamations following the Act of 1964 produced a situation where many local councils felt that their influence over local policing matters had declined.

The recent publicity surrounding the patrol officer and restoring the traditional role of the constable on his beat, together with the need to improve his ability to communicate and maintain contact with the public, tends to overlook the fact that the amalgamations following the Police Act 1964, which reduced the number of police forces in England and Wales to 43, also reduced the capacity of local councils to communicate and maintain contact with their respective chief officers of police. This represented a serious defect in terms of accountability, for chief officers must be responsive to the policing needs and expectations of local communities. The remoteness of some joint police authorities considerably reduced the channels of accountability.

One writer has outlined the principal objection to the creation of larger police forces and larger police authorities.

> They (joint police authorities) are likely to be less rigorous than a committee of a single council, in asserting either their own rights as against the police or those of the constituent units against the Home Office and central government. A combined authority . . . has no civic spirit to stiffen it; no common interest to unite it and no effective local opinion to support it.[11]

The relationship between the independence of the police and their accountability to the public or democratically elected bodies has since been the subject of much debate and no satisfactory answer has been forthcoming. As far as the individual officer is concerned, his legal and constitutional status allows him a wide discretion for which he can be made accountable to the courts or to his superiors under the discipline code. The independence of chief officers, however, in the operational control of their force, is not regulated to the same degree. The accountability which the Royal Commission on the Police stated was of public concern referred to those policing policies which affected the public interest.[12]

The re-organisation of local government in 1974 retained the maintenance and efficiency of the police as a county council or upper tier function which again left a vacuum of accountability in respect of district councils. Contact at this level remained non-statutory and informal and whilst in the majority of cases a satisfactory relationship between the local police and the district council existed, there was no basis for any formal or legal accountability. Consequently, matters of concern could be referred to the county or combined police authority but this was limited by the restriction on police authorities who could only call for reports on the policing of an area and keep themselves informed as to the manner in which complaints were being investigated.

The principle of independence, therefore, must be supported by a satisfactory system of accountability in which the public have confidence especially where there are complaints of arbitrary police action and the infringement of basic liberties. A word of caution is required, however, for a system of accountability under the control of politicians would undermine the authority and independence of chief officers. At the moment they are 'answerable to the law and to the law alone'[13] and there is no evidence to support the suggestion that chief officers abuse this independence. There is nothing to suggest that control exercised by politicians, with little knowledge of professional considerations, would represent a better alternative. Indeed, the recurring example of politicians, both at local and national level, acting out of political or self-interest casts some doubt as to whether the law would be enforced impartially and without fear or favour.

'Independence and accountability' remains a controversial and confused issue but the web becomes less tangled if independence is referable to operational policing policies and practice and accountability is reserved for *ex post facto* investigation and debate. If policies and police practice are open and understood, then there should be no concern on the part of the police if such policies and practices are subjected to the closest scrutiny by those acting in the public interest. The difficulty lies in determining when politicians and others are genuinely acting in the public interest.

Public interest featured in the debate and consultations on the new independent prosecution system recommended by the Royal Commission on Criminal Procedure. The independent aspect of police discretion is discussed in Chapter 4 and this independence has been challenged on several grounds not the least of which is that police decisions are inconsistent and there is no accountability.

Consistency implies fairness, and existing policy guidelines at both national and local level were designed to achieve this as far as possible. Subsequent guidelines issued by the Attorney General sought to achieve greater consistency but the proposed imposition of a *national* prosecution system was no greater guarantee of consistency, even if this was thought consistent with *local* public interest.

This local aspect of public interest, at present safeguarded by the independence of the police, was thought to be vulnerable to local political influence. A working party set up by the Home Secretary in 1982 concluded that the risk of interference by a local supervisory body remained an appreciable one, yet this risk had only arisen from the government's acceptance in principle of the Royal Commission's suggested independent prosecution system. The independence of the police is not affected by any local supervisory system at present.

The subsequent debate on local or national political influence, financial arrangements, organisation and a career structure for the Crown prosecutors clouded the main issue, namely, that the final decision in prosecution cases was being removed from the police and given to an independent body.

Unless there were compelling reasons for doing so, there seemed little purpose in replacing one independent and accountable process with another. The very few cases where the police and the prosecutors hold differing opinions are invariably concerned with police action in response to the public interest. No one can dispute that the quality of the evidence should be determined by legally-qualified solicitors but other non-legal considerations often tilt the balance in favour of or against a prosecution.

The relationship between enforcement of the law and prosecution was referred to in Chapter 4 and it remains to be seen whether a new prosecution system satisfies those critics who doubted the integrity and quality of police decisions. Accountability in prosecution decisions rests with the courts and awards of costs against the prosecutor, the appeal system and a wide range of civil remedies including false imprisonment, or even malicious prosecution. These will remain unchanged whatever the form of any new prosecution system. Any claim, therefore, that there will be greater accountability is doubtful.

The Royal Commission's recommendations for an independent prosecution system may well be seen as a cosmetic exercise to satisfy the notion that justice must be seen to be done even if it is being done already. The Commission found support for their views in the system adopted in British Columbia in 1974 which, it was said, had helped to remove the *suspicion* from the public mind that the system is weighted heavily in favour of the police.[14]

If this has been the purpose – and it may be a necessary ingredient of public confidence – then the erosion of police independence may turn out to have been a heavy price to pay. It is difficult to escape the conclusion that the 'closed' nature of police decisions has been misrepresented as injustice. A shift towards more openness as advocated in Chapter 4 would have been a sufficient measure to allay any public concern, even if this had been based on more than *suspicion*.

The doubtful basis for reform was confirmed by the fact that although the Royal Commission's recommendations were accepted in principle, the fundamental principle of police independence and accountability was being glossed over. The further recommendation that the system should be locally based was rejected in favour of a national system under the superintendence of the Attorney General.

This prompted the natural reaction that local issues and public interest would be ignored. The old conflict between central and local control had been re-opened. Erosion of police independence may have been achieved but the independence of any new system will undoubtedly be challenged, particularly if accountability and responsiveness to local problems proves to be less in evidence than before.

The wider aspects of police accountability can be classed as formal or informal. Formal accountability relates to those statutory measures by which police action can be properly judged and which provide for adequate remedies for those aggrieved. The obvious example of such accountability lies with the law itself. The police are subjected to the same legal constraints as any other person and criminal conduct by a police officer is rightly viewed as a serious matter which may result in criminal proceedings. An investigation may be initiated by a member of the public through the complaints procedure or by a senior police officer if the criminal conduct comes to knowledge from internal sources.

Investigations are carried out by senior police officers and this has caused much critical comment by those who feel that natural justice dictates that the police should not investigate other police officers, the implication being that the impartiality of the investigating officer may be called into question. There is a statutory obligation that allegations of criminal conduct against a police officer which are the subject of complaint by the public must be reported to the Director of Public Prosecutions unless the chief officer is satisfied that no criminal offence has been committed.[15]

The Director of Public Prosecutions, in his evidence to the Royal Commission on Criminal Procedure, said that in practice almost every chief officer was extremely anxious to divest himself of responsibility for deciding whether one of his officers should be prosecuted, however trivial the allegation, so that there could be no suspicion of improper bias. Hence they normally reported all cases involving an officer even if the evidence was virtually non-existent and regardless of whether the complaint had been made by a member of the public.[16]

Formal accountability also extends to breaches of the police discipline code which is also on a statutory basis. A chief officer is required to record and investigate complaints from the public. In some cases it is difficult to ascertain, at the time of complaint, whether the conduct complained of amounts to criminal conduct or a breach of discipline. The investigating officer, therefore, will address his mind to any suspected criminal activity in the first instance as this takes priority over disciplinary matters. The discipline code covers a wide range of improper conduct which can result in disciplinary proceedings. The disciplinary authority, usually the chief constable, before whom the proceedings are held, has a wide range of punishments which can be imposed on an officer ranging from a reprimand or caution to dismissal from the force.

Following the 1964 legislation, which introduced changes in the complaints procedures, the public debate on lack of accountability continued. The main criticism was a lack of any independent element in the procedure which reflected the long-standing objection that the police should not investigate themselves. A post-investigation review of the evidence was one suggestion but this still depended on the quality of the evidence obtained. Proposals put forward in 1974 by the Home Secretary included a system of post-investigation review by an independent body who had the power to decide the outcome of an investigation and these were put on a statutory basis in 1976.

These new statutory measures set up a Police Complaints Board to which a report of every investigation was to be sent, together with a memorandum from the chief officer of police setting out his decision whether to take disciplinary proceedings or not and, where applicable, his reasons for not doing so. The Board had the power to direct that disciplinary proceedings be brought against an officer and they could request that additional information be obtained by further investigation. At first sight, the new system appeared to satisfy the demand for an independent element but criticism continued.

Interested members of the public had been denied the widespread expectation that the Board would have the capacity to examine witnesses or even undertake particular investigations into general complaints against the police as well as specific complaints against individual officers. Criticism of the system also came from the police themselves who, anxious to maintain public confidence, found themselves committed at a senior level to protracted enquiries into comparatively trivial complaints. There was no scope within the system for these minor matters to be resolved informally by local conciliation.

It was felt that many members of the public were genuinely unaware of police practice and procedures and much could be achieved by local discussion and explanation on an informal basis. On the other hand, informal practice of this nature might lend itself to abuse and the true extent of public complaint could not be monitored. There is a tendency, also, as identified by the Director of Public Prosecutions, for the police to be anxious to demonstrate their impartiality and objectivity in investigations by an insistence on a thorough investigation into any matter of complaint. The benefit is public confidence in the police service and in the integrity of the investigation process. The burden is a sapping of morale at street level where the patrol officer finds it hard to understand why a senior officer is able to devote more time to investigating police conduct than he, himself, is able to devote to investigating serious complaints of crime.

This imbalance becomes even more unacceptable when it is realised that the majority of the complaints are unfounded or unsubstantiated. It is well recognised, even outside of police circles, that many complaints are in response to arrest or other legal process and an attempt is made to discredit the police officer on whose evidence a prosecution will be based. Invariably, the matter complained of is so closely associated with the circumstances of the arrest or offence that a formal investigation is postponed under the *sub judice* rule. During the court hearing of the main issue, it is a recurring tactic by the defence to confirm before the court that a complaint has been made against the officer. Since the matter has not been investigated at that stage, this tactic is questionable and offends natural justice. The judicial process is not sufficiently refined to accept such a statement without prejudice.

The problems associated with complaints arising from arrest have been recognised by the Police Complaints Board who commented that they were satisfied that some allegations of assault made by persons facing charges were without substance and had been made with the objective of discrediting the police and gaining the sympathy of the court.[17]

Despite the introduction of an independent element into the system of investigating complaints, criticism persisted and gradually increased as the ineffectiveness of the Police Complaints Board became apparent. This ineffectiveness lay in the fact that the most serious allegations, usually involving violence, were still being investigated by the police and reported to the Director of Public Prosecutions in the normal way. The real objection was that with no independent element in the investigative stage, there were no safeguards which would ensure that all available evidence was obtained.

The Police Complaints Board, in its first triennial review of the revised system did not share this concern and were satisfied that in the vast majority of cases which came before them, a thorough and fair investigation had been made by the police into the complainant's allegations, and although this might not have revealed the whole truth, it had provided all available evidence on which to make a proper adjudication.[18]

Those who did not share the Board's confidence in the impartiality and effectiveness of the police investigation failed to realise that the more serious allegations against police officers involve allegations of criminal conduct and the only body charged with the responsibility of investigating crime are the police. The Board, in outlining the practical difficulties associated with the imposition of an independent investigative body, pointed out that it would be necessary to invest the members of a lay body with the powers of a constable and that relevant information would be in the possession of the police. It was difficult to envisage the source from which any lay investigators could be recruited and the Board doubted whether schemes, like the Dutch system, which utilises the investigative experience of retired police officers would overcome the objections based on impartiality.

Those who criticise the existing system also appear to overlook the real difficulties facing an investigator, whether he be a police officer or anyone else. The main difficulty is one of evidence or, more precisely, the sufficiency of evidence. The Police Complaints Board drew attention to the limitation of available evidence where there were allegations of violence against police officers. They said that assaults which were alleged to have occurred during arrest or while in custody were unlikely to be witnessed by civilians and where there was a denial supported by one or more police colleagues and no corroborative evidence to support the allegation neither criminal nor disciplinary action against a police officer was likely.[19]

Lord Scarman also commented on this issue and said:

One constant problem – which no procedural change can overcome – is that many complaints resolve themselves into a conflict of evidence between the complainant and the accused police officer, with no third element present which could objectively resolve the conflict. This situation is, of course, common in a court of law, but whereas few feel aggrieved if a defendant is acquitted because of lack of evidence, someone complaining against the police is unlikely to accept a similar 'not guilty' verdict – . . . whatever the system for considering complaints, none is going to satisfy all complainants or silence all critics.[20]

Lord Scarman had reviewed the police complaints procedure in connection with his enquiry into the Brixton riots. He identified the main criticisms as a lack of confidence in the impartiality and fairness of the procedure, the formality of the system in dealing with relatively minor complaints and that the existing system did not cater for complaints against policing policies but only against individual misconduct. In addition, there was evidence that letters to complainants were unhelpful and that the 'double jeopardy' rule[21] precluded any disciplinary action if the evidence submitted to the Director of Public Prosecutions was insufficient for criminal proceedings.

His suggestions for reform included the introduction of an independent investigation service or a 'non-police' supervisor. He also advocated a conciliation process for minor complaints and he felt that complaints of a general nature could be accommodated by a more vigorous exercise of a police authority's existing powers, together with the involvement of local consultative or liaison committees.

The Home Secretary, in accepting Lord Scarman's criticisms, stated that the procedure for handling complaints against the police must be substantially reformed if it was to command public confidence.[22]

Subsequent proposals[23] recommended a three-tier system which would operate according to the seriousness of the allegation. The most serious allegations involving death or serious injury would be investigated by a senior police officer normally from an outside force under the supervision of an independent assessor who would ensure that the investigation was done expeditiously, thoroughly and impartially. The second tier would apply to complaints of a substantial nature which would continue to be investigated by a senior officer and referred to the Police Complaints Board for independent review. The principal variation would be that complaints involving allegations of minor criminal offences would no longer be automatically referable to the Director of Public Prosecutions.

Minor complaints of a less serious nature would be subject to an informal procedure and this third tier would include an element of conciliation. This informal procedure would require the agreement of the complainant and if the matter could not be resolved informally, a formal investigation would be undertaken under the second-tier procedure.

The whole emphasis was on greater accountability and a greater degree of confidence in the complaints system. The government felt that a more flexible system would be more responsive to the wishes of the complainant but it remained firm on the principle of independence. They reaffirmed that the primary responsibility for the maintenance of discipline within his force should remain in the hands of the chief officer.[24] It was also emphasised that there could be no question of seeking greater acceptance of complaints procedures at the cost of sacrificing the legitimate rights of police officers. Confidence in the complaints system was an important aspect of the relationship between the police and public generally, but it had to be enjoyed by both parties to the relationship if the system was to work satisfactorily.[25]

During the subsequent debate, however, it was felt that these measures did not go far enough. Further proposals favoured a new Police Complaints Authority instead of an independent assessor.[26] This new Authority, which would replace the existing Police Complaints Board, would have much wider powers within a system which seemed to accommodate a four-tier structure.

The first-tier represented those serious allegations involving death or serious injury in which the Authority would be required to supervise and control the investigation. A second-tier would involve other allegations of varying degrees of seriousness where the Authority would have a discretion as to whether it should be involved in the investigation or not. A chief officer of police would be required to notify the Authority of such complaints and this category would also involve other complaints where the chief officer considered the Authority should be informed under a system of discretionary notification. The criteria for such cases would include the need to reassure the public that a full and proper investigation was being made.

Where investigations were not supervised by the Authority, allegations would either be resolved by a normal investigation or by informal resolution. The object behind the proposals was a new system of investigating complaints which would enjoy the confidence of both the police and the public. Various changes were advocated in respect of better representation for accused officers. Procedural changes were intended to streamline procedures and lead to a better use of police resources.

The police, themselves, recognised that some change would be necessary in the complaints system. The introduction of an independent element into the investigatory stage may well prove an important measure which removes any doubt that the police have not carried out their investigations in a full and professional manner. Where allegations or criticism are unfair or unfounded, it will be of some assurance to both police and public that there will be an independent recognition of malicious, vindictive and frivolous complaints which puts the quality of police performance into perspective.

As far as the individual officer is concerned, the complaints system represents one element, and perhaps the most important, of formal accountability. He is accountable to the criminal law and can be held liable at civil law for a variety of actions such as assault, negligence and false imprisonment. He is subjected to a rigorous discipline code which can render him liable to dismissal in serious cases of misconduct. The discipline code can also be used to deal with any failure to observe force orders and procedures.

On an informal basis, he is accountable to his immediate supervisory officers in connection with his day to day duties but it is often overlooked that an officer is also accountable to himself. His own discretion and independence of action can often be measured against a service ideal or the public expectation of his role.

It could be said that formal accountability should relate more to the individual officer than to the general policies of chief officers for it is the individual officer who is in contact with the public and who may be subjected to the greatest criticism. His independence of action and discretion are well regulated and numerous safeguards exist to protect the public from arbitrary action.[27]

At chief officer level, a greater degree of independence exists for he is not subjected to supervision and his policy making function is more remote from the public. This remoteness can often be the greatest source of criticism for there has been an increasing demand for more accountability in respect of general policing policies. The saturation policing operation in Brixton which has already been referred to, perhaps demonstrated the jealously guarded view that politicians or the public had no contribution to make in respect of operational policing policies.

Lord Scarman thought otherwise. 'Community involvement in the policy and operations of policing is perfectly feasible without undermining the independence of the police or destroying the secrecy of those operations against crime which have to be kept secret.'[28] He considered that the police at Brixton could have consulted community leaders before embarking on a saturation operation in a sensitive area. He did not support the view that consultation would have threatened the success of the operation and intruded upon their independence of judgement as senior police officers.[29]

He concluded that 'Consultation and accountability are the mechanisms – in part administrative, and in part legal – upon which we rely to ensure that the police in their policies and operations keep in touch with, and are responsible to, the community they police.'[30] It is significant that in describing the existing links between accountability and consultation, Lord Scarman dealt separately with the Metropolitan Police District and other areas outside London.

At the centre of the whole issue of police accountability is the role of the Home Secretary. As the Police Authority for the Metropolitan Police he is in a unique position which effectively rules out any local accountability except where issues are raised in Parliament. Outside London, the respective police authorities are local in character and have statutory functions to which I have already referred.[31] A police authority can require a chief constable to submit a report in writing on specified matters and he is obliged to do so unless the information required ought not to be disclosed in the public interest or is not within the scope of the police authority's function.[32]

It had long been recognised that many police authorities did not make full use of their statutory powers and it seems that many were uncertain of the extent to which they could interfere with a chief officer's operational independence. In any event, Lord Scarman drew attention to the fact that in discharging their responsibilities to maintain an adequate and efficient police force, some police authorities were uncertain of their powers and had not acted with sufficient firmness. He emphasised that they had a duty to exercise these powers and he was in no doubt that a police force which did not consult locally could be regarded as inefficient.[33]

The principal criticism of the existing arrangements was that there was no duty imposed on police authorities to ensure that consultative machinery was established between the police and the community at all levels. A chief officer could discuss general issues with his police authority but it was at local divisional and sub-divisional levels where a vacuum of liaison existed.

Lord Scarman saw the solution in the imposition of a statutory duty on police authorities and chief officers to co-operate in establishing and supervising liaison committees and other local consultative bodies. In many areas of the country this must have been received with some surprise since police officers at all levels had enjoyed close co-operation and consultation with their respective local councils and community representatives for many years.[34]

Liaison with the community can operate, therefore, in a variety of ways which reflect the levels of responsibility. Thus, a chief officer can consult with and be responsive to his police authority; a divisional or sub-divisional commander to his local district council and a beat officer to his parish council. There is nothing new about this form of informal consultation. In urban areas, the area beat officer has developed links with residents' associations and other local bodies and it has been generally understood that such a relationship has many benefits. What is now being suggested is that the existing structure should be developed so that local policing objectives can be identified and influenced by community involvement. Influence is not the same as interference and does not undermine independence.[35]

What is questionable is whether consultative machinery should be imposed on a statutory basis since it is clear that much has been achieved already quite voluntarily. As a result of the riots and disorders in urban areas, formal accountability in the shape of consultation was being imposed on informal arrangements which in many areas had already established good relationships between the local police and the public. The difficulty with a statutory duty to consult was that it imposed a general duty where none was required.

Several points emerge from this. Firstly, the matters on which Lord Scarman was basing his recommendations occurred in the Metropolitan Police District which has no locally appointed police authority. Secondly, the existing pattern of consultation at all levels in many forces outside London, does not include the wider concept of accountability envisaged by Lord Scarman. A further point is whether a statutory duty to consult can really be effective.

It is perhaps surprising that Lord Scarman did not recommend any fundamental change in the nature of the police authority for the Metropolitan Police area given that so much of the evidence he heard pointed towards a rationalisation of the structures in London and elsewhere. Although he recommended a statutory framework of local consultation between the borough councils in London and the respective local police districts he avoided the central area of criticism.

The point being urged was that local ratepayers outside of London enjoyed a channel of communication through their local police authority and, to some extent, had a degree of influence on policing matters. The additional statutory measures suggested by Lord Scarman would also provide for local liaison committees at district council and other levels in these areas thus offering a further opportunity for influencing policies on policing. This would result in consultative machinery being developed in provincial areas outside London, while in the capital itself there was no structure at police authority level for community involvement and influence.

Since the nation's attention had been focused on Brixton and the apparent break-down in community relations at Lambeth, it was thought that some recommendations might have been made which would have established consultation and accountability on a wider level than proposed. As far as the London boroughs were concerned, Lord Scarman recommended a statutory framework whereby local consultative and liaison committees would consist, not only of local police officers, but councillors and representatives of other community groups.

He considered it essential that they should be given powers in such matters as the complaints procedure, inspection of detention areas in police stations and a right of referral to a new Metropolitan Police Advisory Board. This proposed Board would consist of representatives from the Home Office and it seemed to be an attempt to merge the present authority of the Home Secretary with some element of local representation.[36]

Subsequently, the Home Secretary issued guidelines on how

consultative arrangements could be implemented by utilising the existing statutory powers of chief constables and police authorities. The emphasis was on contact between the police and the community at local level and it was suggested that many local organisations could be represented to good effect. The object was for police authorities to develop their role with the support of consultation so that policies could be implemented which identified needs in the light of expressed concern by the local community.[37]

There remains a doubt about the effectiveness of statutory consultative measures since meaningful consultation includes a willingness by all concerned to discuss issues and seek solutions. In some areas, it is clear that a lack of confidence or trust will persist and these barriers will have to be broken down patiently with rational discussion. Attitudes, prejudice and ignorance are often the reasons why barriers exist and although statutory measures may achieve the existence of consultative committees, it is only the willingness of those concerned to understand the issues involved which will make such consultation effective. Statutory measures will not change attitudes and there was nothing to suggest that the existing consultative machinery, even in London, had failed other than by an unwillingness of those concerned to change or modify their views.

The principle of independence and accountability, therefore, cannot be considered without regard to the further element of consultation but it is essential that these three concepts are fully understood. Lord Scarman rightly pointed out that the independence of the police means operational independence. Accountability is a necessary ingredient for two reasons – it ensures that the police act responsibly and it ensures that the police act on behalf of the community. Consultation is the process whereby policing can be responsive to the identified needs of the community. The long debate which followed Lord Scarman's report really centred on those matters which could properly form the basis for consultation. The real issue under discussion was the relationship between operational independence and political independence.

To the majority of police officers, the issue presents little difficulty since they are aware that they are prevented by regulations from taking any active part in politics.[38] The basis for this regulation is that the police must remain impartial. They are servants of the law and not of governments. There was growing concern, however, over an attempt by some police authorities to influence operational policing policies. It was claimed that such attempts were not always being made in the public interest since the obvious target appeared to be the operational independence of chief officers.

One chief officer was prompted to publicly state his concern at what he saw as a serious attempt to subvert and demoralise the police and to destroy its traditional and proven structure.[39] His reference to a 'dangerous, insidious and ruthless enemy' drew criticism from every shade of political opinion but he considered that police authorities should be abolished and replaced by non-political police boards who would act objectively in the public interest.

The Commissioner of the Metropolitan Police, on taking up office in 1982, was also prompted to point out the difficulties facing the police where the political climate was 'inimical to progress'. Objective proposals for change in the control over the police became lost in a 'campaign of dedicated denigration' which included uneducated and unfair criticism, accompanied by 'zealous dredging for any incident that (could) be exploited as a cause celebre'.

The distortion of public opinion and expectations was also the subject of comment. The Commissioner referred to the practice of representing any police intervention as 'harassment' and emphasised the real danger that 'these activists gain publicity for their views out of all proportion to their influence in the community'.[40]

It is difficult for chief officers to offer views publicly on such matters since they are then entering the political arena themselves. On the other hand silence indicates agreement with the view that there should be a greater degree of political control over policing policies. The pattern of consultative arrangements set out by the Home Secretary and which embrace the various groups at local level provides some optimism for the future. Chief officers and police authorities would then have available to them a wide body of local opinion on many issues which would influence and enhance the quality of decision making with regard to policing policies as they affect the community as a whole.

The Home Secretary envisaged the involvement, not only of democratically elected bodies such as district and parish councils, but also of residents' associations, youth organisations, church councils, educational establishments and any responsible groups who could contribute to discussions on local issues. The advantages of such arrangements would be that liaison and consultative committees would emerge which were representative of local communities but which were non-political in nature. The independence of chief officers in operational matters would be preserved but their independence of action would be responsive to local needs and their policies could reflect local opinion or concern on identified problems.

The strength of such arrangements would lie in the fact that they would be voluntary and not statutory, informal rather than formal, and they would reflect a willingness by those involved to seek the common good. Here we can identify traces of the ancient collective responsibility for law and order which was one of the earliest principles of policing.

It was stressed that while the police were charged with the prevention of crime and the maintenance of order, those tasks could not be fulfilled effectively unless the community itself shouldered its responsibilities for tackling the particular problems of an area. Arrangements for local consultation between police and community ought to focus on local problems. He added that in order to make a reality of community involvement, consultation should reach into the local community, draw in the people who live there and reflect the views of their own neighbourhood.

Perhaps the last word in independence and accountability can be found in some important and perceptive comments by an acknowledged authority on comparative policing systems. In a lecture on leadership in the police service,[41] he referred to the two large-scale re-structurings of the police which had produced larger forces and which had, in many instances, severed the roots from which public support and co-operation had traditionally come. He saw political influence as a threat to the independence of the police and commented, 'If the police are ever seen as the agents of the majority party in either central or local government . . . the impartiality and the respect without which police in democratic countries cannot function effectively will be irretrievably lost.'

He also emphasised the extent to which the police were already accountable to public opinion, the Home Secretary, the local authority and, above all, to the law. He felt that the public did not understand this sufficiently and reiterated that any political involvement in operational control of the police would endanger the independence on which professional integrity depends. He did not believe that the great majority of the public desired any change and added, 'I suspect that most of them have a better opinion of police than they have of politicians.' He concluded that the strength and success of British policing rested in the historic office of constable with its responsibilities and its scope for independence and discretion.

This reinforces the view that discretion has an important influence on the independence of the police and there is a further indication here of the key to effective policing which was discussed in connection with discretion – openness. If policing policies are open and formulated in response to open debate by consultative machinery; if police practice is open in that the public understand the reasons why the police act in the way they do; if police procedures are open to review; if policing issues and problems are open to debate, then the public interest will be served and accountability enhanced.

9 The Application of Principles

Since the inception of the modern police service, there have been several attempts to set out the various principles of policing[1] but the most recent re-statement of principle can be found in Lord Scarman's Report on the Brixton Disorders which has been quoted at length in earlier chapters. The two basic principles of 'consent and balance' and 'independence and accountability' represent the essence of effective policing and it is significant that when the police service was faced with a crisis and was being subjected to wide criticism, Lord Scarman felt compelled to judge the actions of the police against a background of principle.[2]

It is fashionable to refer to traditional policing principles as a cure for the apparent ills which afflict the modern service. These traditional principles, however, have not always been recognised or fully understood. In earlier chapters, the principle of local and collective responsibility for law and order was emphasised as an historical link with the Anglo-Saxon period but this principle has been challenged as being based on 'a certain historical sentimentality'.[3] This theme was taken up by Professor Goodhart in his dissenting memorandum in the final report of the Royal Commission on the Police in 1962.[4] He identified six principles which the Commission had adopted as a basis for preserving the local character of the police and his comments, intended to support his claim for regional police forces, demonstrate how important it is to try to analyse principles which in themselves appear deceptively simple.

The first principle he doubted was that being a direct descendant of the parish constable, the modern constable held an independent office, not subject to superior control. This principle has been the basis for the independence of chief officers and Professor Goodhart commented that their ambition to claim the honour of having the parish constable as an ancestor 'seemed an odd one as his contemporaries had nothing but evil to speak of him'.[5]

The next three principles touched on the local character of the police, the partnership between local and central government and the impartiality of the police. Professor Goodhart doubted the Commission's understanding of these principles and his criticisms were directed at the main target of attack which was the unfettered power of chief constables.[6] The fifth principle concerning the consent and co-operation of the public he regarded as of more recent origin and he felt that the most important factor in obtaining the support and the confidence of the public was that the police should be as efficient as possible. To this extent, he thought that the police should not rest on their past reputation but should be reorganised to meet present day needs. Finally, he found it hard to accept the constitutional and political arguments against a regional or national police force and that they would pose a threat to liberty. He stated, 'The danger in a democracy does not lie in a central police that is too strong but in local police forces that are too weak.'[7]

Professor Goodhart's attack on traditional principles was not necessarily directed at the nature of the principles themselves, but that too much emphasis had been placed on those principles which were claimed to have their origin in the pre-1829 period. He rightly points out that the pre-1829 period was not a Golden Age in which there was respect and support for the police and states, 'It was not until the Metropolitan Police proved that they could maintain law and order that they gained, first the respect, and then the affection of the people.'[8]

However, in recognising the inspiration of Peel that an unarmed force could still maintain peace and good order, he failed to emphasise that Peel's real inspiration was in retaining the office and common law powers of the former constable. It was the traditional nature of the office, not its efficiency, which enabled Peel to overcome the constitutional and political objections of that time. Once the new police had been established, it was Rowan and Mayne who applied themselves to the problems of efficiency.

If efficiency had been Peel's main consideration, he would not have faithfully retained the traditional subordination of the constable to the justices since this had long proved itself to be an inefficient structure. However, the new Commissioners, although justices, acted under the Secretary of State and a degree of central supervision was imposed. The development of the provincial police forces followed a different path and it was not until 1888 that the control by the justices in rural areas was finally replaced by a joint committee of justices and councillors when the new county councils were created.

It can be argued, therefore, that while the historical traditions of 'keeping the peace' were faithfully retained and embodied in the new police systems of the nineteenth century, the development of the service has been not only influenced by particular principles but fettered by them. It is perhaps surprising that the recommendations of a Royal Commission in 1839 that police forces in the counties should be under the ultimate control of Parliament in the same way as the Metropolitan Police were rejected. Political influence and control seemed to be a greater priority than efficient police forces under parliamentary supervision.

The path of reform outlined in Chapter 1 illustrates the subsequent conflict between locally controlled police forces and central supervision, exercised by an inspectorate acting under the authority of the Home Secretary. It can be argued that the reforms brought about by the Police Act 1964 were not radical enough and the result was a compromise between the former diversity of local forces and a degree of regional or national control. The difficulty in promoting radical reform does lie with an understanding of the application of traditional principles. Traditional principles have become blurred with traditional functions surrounding the office of constable and it is perhaps best to confine traditional principles to those which were embodied in the new police of 1829. The traditional office and powers of the constable were retained, not as a matter of principle, but as a *function* in order that the new professional police would be accepted by the public and constitutional and political objections would be avoided. To this extent, the historical origins of the office were embodied in the principle of policing by consent.

It was this issue of consent which gave the British police its unique quality since the nature of policing had to be acceptable to the public. It was emphasised during the early days of the new police that they should be helpful rather than oppressive and the application of the principle of minimum force supported this mild, persuasive style of policing. It was recognised that the public would only consent to the use of force when the force used was the minimum necessary to achieve the objective and in many cases it would be unnecessary for force to be used at all.

The principle of policing by consent also extended into the whole field of police conduct and to the manner in which they carried out their duties. The earlier chapters on police ethics, police discretion and police sensitivity illustrate the difficulties involved in reconciling the coercive nature of policing with the public acceptance of their role. They also provide an insight into the many ways in which the police can improve their level of performance to meet the high standards expected of them.

It was not surprising, therefore, that Lord Scarman should stress the importance of the principle of policing by consent and its relationship with a balanced approach to law enforcement. Much emphasis was placed on the need to consult with the community and to involve them in police initiatives to deal with local problems. This and other recommendations by Lord Scarman touched on the other basic principle of independence and accountability. It is clear that the application of these two basic principles by Lord Scarman represented a thorough re-appraisal of the police role in society. The result was a predictable response by the police themselves to undertake a detailed self-examination. Police training was reviewed and in particular the problems associated with community and race relations.

It was said that the distinction between community and race relations should be retained although this distinction had been criticised as projecting race as being separate from community relations. It is felt that if a conscious effort is made to ensure that a proper relationship exists between the police and the community then race should only become an issue in those areas which are multi-racial in character. Furthermore by treating them separately it suggests that minority ethnic groups are a special problem or are being specially favoured.

Nevertheless, it was decided to retain the distinction.

It is not simply that the most difficult and intractable problems between the police and the public arise where race is an issue; it is rather that racial and cultural differences can introduce complexities of a special nature and order into encounters between individuals and groups.[9]

In recognising the need for community and race relations

training, emphasis was placed on the wider role of the police in society and the dangers associated with the view, prevalent in inner-city areas, that the police task is more or less exclusively one of law enforcement.

> Such a narrow conception of their role can lead officers to exercise their discretion without regard to the effect of their actions on long-term relations with the public and to regard themselves as representing an authority apart from the community.[10]

It was concluded that training should be aimed at both attitudes and behaviour with the objective of enhancing the effectiveness of the police. It should reflect local requirements and focus on the day to day aspects of policing together with a knowledge of the local community. In addition, training would be given in human and racism awareness and behavioural skills in dealing with the public.[11]

A comprehensive review was also undertaken of the training required by probationer constables and a list of broad objectives were drawn up which reinforced the principle of consent and illustrates how British policing responded to the recommendations in Lord Scarman's Report. It also demonstrated how police training emerged from the former rigid mould of law and procedure to a recognition that a police officer requires a much wider conception of his role and extensive training in those skills which enable him to be effective in dealing with the public.

These broad objectives included a re-statement of the principle of policing with consent and that training should reflect the need for police officers to secure the approval, confidence and respect of the community. This re-affirms the original instruction to police officers in 1829 that 'much depends on the approval and co-operation of the public and these have always been determined by the degree of the esteem and respect in which the police are held'.

The objectives also included, for the first time, the notion of a 'professional ethic' which was defined as a 'firm commitment to established and implicit human rights and the maintenance of high ethical standards'. This is essentially a postscript to Chapter 3 and reflects the need for a code of ethics as an essential basis for all aspects of the policing function.

Lord Scarman's view that British policing had not yet adjusted to the problems of policing a multi-racial society was reflected in the inclusion of social awareness as an objective for probationer training. This was linked to the recommendations on community and race relations training and recognised that an understanding of the various cultural backgrounds and attitudes was essential. Research had indicated that hostile attitudes arose not from inherent prejudice but from actual street experience.[12] The attitude and behaviour of superiors was considered beneficial to young officers to whom the impact of training was minimal compared with the impact of socialisation within the group. This 'peer pressure' has already been commented on[13] and it was found that officers would often use derogatory language in order to conform with their colleagues. It was noted that police officers believed strongly in learning by experience and were very sceptical about the value of training.

A further broad objective of training refers to preventive skills to prevent disorder and to defuse situations of potential conflict. This reinforces the principle of prevention and arose from the evidence presented to Lord Scarman during his enquiry. This objective also recognises the need to train police officers in the use of protective shields and other defensive measures. The reference to defensive measures is in contrast to the offensive measures widely adopted in other parts of the world to deal with serious outbreaks of disorder. It reflects the principle of minimum force and reference was made to 'the professional use of force to enable people to be restrained with least possible harm'.

Emphasis was also placed on the need for officers to acquire an adequate understanding of human interactions and relationships and to be able to apply inter-personal skills in the course of their duties. This could be regarded as a postscript to the chapter on 'sense and sensitivity' which identified those areas where skills in matters such as communication and crisis intervention are essential and which also referred to the need for officers to recognise their prejudices and attitudes.

The collective effect of these broad objectives for probationer training should be significant for they emphasise the complexities of modern policing yet are based on traditional principles which have stood the test of time. In addition, they illustrate the increasing demands made on individual officers and the professional image to which they should aspire. It is equally important that these broad objectives are applied to the training of all officers whose own development has not been influenced by the wider social considerations of an enlightened approach to effective policing.

The application of traditional principles to police training is not sufficient if the theory is not supported by practice. It is often difficult to reconcile the genuine concern for the relationship between the police and the public with the lack of recognition within the service to the role of the patrol officer who is best placed to cultivate and develop the essential link with the public at street level. The decline in the status of the patrol officer undoubtedly stems from the increase in specialisation. Although this reflected the growing complexities of modern policing, the result was that more and more officers knew less and less about the basic police function and the necessary skills required by the patrol officer.

It has also been widely recognised that the various schemes of mobile policing, which were introduced on economic grounds when recruitment levels were low, also had its impact on the traditional nature of policing. The original schemes of mobile policing were designed to combine both the advantages of mobility with the patrol function and it was an integral part of such schemes that officers should patrol on foot at different locations. However, the availability of mobile patrols to deal with increasing incidents tended to result in full time mobile patrol duties and there was little scope for the basic patrol function. One obvious effect was to minimise the opportunities for police officers to communicate with and cultivate a relationship with the public on the streets.

There is now a clear reversal of this trend and much emphasis is being placed on returning police officers to foot patrol. Whilst this return to traditional methods of patrolling the beat has been widely acknowledged by the public, it must be asked why the status of the beat officer was allowed to decline. His role had become devalued because the service had tended to overlook the essential nature of policing. The true distinction between prevention and detection had become obscured and there had been a confusion between function and principle.

The detection of crime is merely a function but the control of crime and disorder relies on the principle of prevention. Too much emphasis is placed on the fanatical pursuit of the impossible – a high level of detection. Whilst the detection of crime is an important aspect of the police role, the true test of police efficiency lies in their capacity to prevent crime and disorder. The general instructions to the police in 1829 emphasised that, 'the absence of crime will be considered the best proof of the complete efficiency of the Police.'

The noted historian, Charles Reith, regarded this as a principle in itself, namely, that the test of police efficiency is the absence of crime and disorder and not the visible evidence of police action in dealing with them.[14] It is easy to conclude that such a view is outdated and not in step with the complexities and pressures of modern urban policing but the value of this principle is at last being recognised. Some specialist squads are being disbanded and officers returned to patrol duties. Other measures are being adopted which, although done in the name of community policing, are really based on the preventive principle.

This in itself is insufficient. What is required is a fundamental change of attitude by the police themselves to the role of the beat officer. He is the officer who is the true professional and the importance of his role must be given the recognition it deserves. If there is genuine concern about the public and a more responsive approach to policing problems in the community, it surely cannot be right that the most important role in the service, the contact point with the public, is often left to the youngest, most inexperienced and, in some cases, the least motivated officers.

This is not to deny that there are many outstanding patrol officers who excel in their role and derive much satisfaction from helping the community but in a predominantly young service, the guiding influence of the mature and experienced officer has declined. Sound judgement and the art of discretion cannot be learned overnight. The failure to give proper attention to the development of young officers is compounded by the apparent urge to specialise at the first opportunity. It is difficult to escape the conclusion that the police culture identifies beat duty as merely a starting point for better things.

Another conclusion which can be drawn is that some officers tend to seek specialist duties which hold more attraction than the rigours of street duty. The unsocial hours, continuous supervision, the physical demands and stress arising from street incidents and vulnerability to assault, together with the routine nature of the work, cannot compete with the glamour of the specialist who is often accorded undue prominence within the police structure and is often remote from the 'wear and tear' of operational life.

The increasing complexities of police work and the many technological advances in recent years have dictated a wider need for specialisation in the police service but they have also tended to obscure the fundamental role of the patrol officer. The true professional is the officer who has recognised the service aspect of his role; who has mastered the art of policing at street level; who can relate to the community he serves and who can respond effectively and sensitively to the variety of problems that arise.

Lord Scarman recognised the importance of the officer at street level and urged that the status of the beat officer would have to be enhanced if policing was to be effective.

> He must, in my view, be seen not as occupying the bottom of the police pecking-order (after the CID and specialist units have creamed off the best), but at its apex, in the forefront of the police team. Policing, like medicine, the law and the civil service, is a profession in which the general practitioner is as necessary as the specialist.[15]

If the general practitioner is to be effective, then it is essential that he is given sufficient training to equip him for his role and to enable him to deal with the complexities of modern policing. In the past, there has been an assumption that the young officer will learn the art of street duty from his mature colleagues but street training programmes have suffered from a lack of experienced officers. However, the influence of mature officers is not always for the good. Careful selection of tutor constables, who themselves may require special training, is an important aspect in the development of a young officer.

In trying to shape the attitudes and influence the behaviour of young officers, however, it is important to recognise that they have a special value by virtue of their age. Lord Scarman commented that young police officers were not only unavoidable, but valuable. He had no doubt they had a role to play which an older officer could not understudy. He pointed out that for younger officers, no generation gap existed to separate them from young people on the streets and that they shared with them recent school experience, had the same interests and had the same personal problems. He added that age in itself was certainly no guarantee of wisdom and that young officers should not be removed from sensitive areas but should receive proper guidance and supervision in discharging their difficult delicate and indispensable function.[16]

In earlier chapters, comment has been made on the limitations which existed in the initial training for police officers in this country and this was reflected in Lord Scarman's recommendations for increased training and an extension of the initial training course to six months.[17] He pointed out that a recruit to a British police force received a good deal less training than his counterpart in a number of other countries. He could not see how the existing arrangements could adequately cover the increasing complexities of a police officer's task.[18]

In the United States, an officer in most of the large urban police departments receives six months initial training. This includes firearms training and an intensive physical fitness programme. From my own knowledge of the training programme for the New York Police Department, many of the matters suggested by Lord Scarman as the underlying theme of a recruit's initial training were included in American recruit training programmes many years ago.

It is clear that their own serious urban disturbances some years ago prompted a review of initial police training and their current programmes cover a wide variety of subjects which place the policing role in perspective and demonstrate how police professionalism has developed in that country. An officer will learn about philosophy, policing in a democracy, the nature of his authority and the importance of integrity and ethics. He will also study psychology, personality and behaviour, attitudes, prejudice, communication, crisis intervention and victimology.

Much emphasis is placed on the nature of patrol work, an officer's professional image and his relationship with the public. It is significant that the British police service is drawing more and more on American sources for advice and assistance with police training although these sources have been there for some years. There has been a marked reluctance to concede that anything can be learned from American policing methods but that is to deny the extent of police professionalism in that country.

Human awareness, crisis intervention, communication and other associated subjects are now being accepted as important aspects of policing modern society because they give an officer the basis to develop practical skills in dealing with people. The British police service has now recognised that the important principle of policing with consent was in danger of being eroded. Technological advances and a pre-occupation with organisation, management and administrative matters had produced a tendency to look inwards and to ignore and fail to recognise changes in the social climate.

As Lord Scarman commented:

> Technological advances have offered new ways of preventing and fighting crime, of protecting life and property, and of quelling disorder without the necessity of maintaining close personal relations with the community. Indeed, not the least of the problems the police now face is how to take advantage of their technological aids without destroying the human factor, so essential if policing is to command public support.[19]

The earlier chapters on ethics, discretion and sensitivity are all concerned with the human factor and the need to adopt a balanced view of law enforcement. Police training has traditionally concentrated on police powers and enforcement since these are essential areas of study. If this is supplemented by a professional approach to enforcement and policing generally which recognises the stresses in society and the wider means of achieving objectives, then the role of the police officer will be enhanced and the principle of consent more widely understood.

The application of this principle to the sphere of training is not sufficient in itself for there are many police officers who have been serving for many years without the benefit of this wider appreciation of their role. Many have learned from experience or acquired skills based on the experiences of others and there is a clear need for internal policies and directives to reflect the principles under discussion. It may often be necessary to reiterate these principles as a justification for policy so that officers can understand the basic rationale of policy decisions.

The principle of policing by consent is also affected by the principle of minimum force which has already been discussed at some length. The public consent to the use of force as a lawful means of securing compliance but the force used must only be the minimum necessary to achieve the objective. The principle also recognises that there are many situations where no force is necessary at all and the objective can be achieved quite easily by persuasion and advice. There is little doubt that the use of unnecessary or excessive force provokes considerable public hostility towards the police and, in extreme cases, can undermine the whole structure of police and public relations.

It is only right, therefore, and widely accepted by all responsible police officers that allegations of assault committed by police officers should be the subject of rigorous investigation. The vulnerability of persons in custody is a natural cause for concern and it is difficult to reassure the public in view of the closed nature of procedures and practices in police stations. This lack of openness and accountability has prompted proposals for lay visitors to police stations and greater safeguards against police abuse. Lord Scarman felt that more could be done with regard to the safeguards for suspected persons under interrogation or detention in police stations. He recommended that members of police committees and the proposed new consultative committees should have a right to visit police stations at any time and to report on what they observed. He felt such measures would strengthen local accountability and would have a salutary effect on police procedures.[20]

In discussing accountability, the over-riding consideration is to maintain public confidence in the police system. Incidents of misconduct, where substantiated, should attract appropriate penalties as the police service, like any other profession, must demonstrate that it is competent and capable of correcting and deterring deviations from its own accepted standard of conduct.

The principles identified and discussed in previous chapters are not exhaustive but are those which appear to be fundamental to the nature and continued existence of traditional policing. They represent the way in which a constitutional democracy has managed to solve the historical problem of reconciling the police function with the interests of society and the freedom of the individual.

The recurring problem was essentially a conflict between utilitarian and libertarian principles. What emerged was a series of compromises between different philosophies, theories and principles. The issue was clearly expressed by the Royal Commission on the Police in 1962 who stated that it was in the public interest:

> that the police should be strong and effective in preserving law and order and preventing crime; but it is equally to the public

good that police power should be controlled and confined so as not to interfere arbitrarily with personal freedom. The result is compromise. The police should be powerful but not oppressive; they should be efficient but not officious; they should form an impartial force in the body politic, and yet be subject to a degree of control by persons who are not required to be impartial and who themselves are liable to police supervision.[21]

The art of compromise is nothing more than a balancing act and the application of basic policing principles will often tip the balance in the right direction. The difficulty with a word like compromise is that it has the appearance of being the best or worst of both worlds so that some will view a particular trend as soft or weak whilst others will see it as harsh or oppressive. It is important that the views of both sides are understood and openly discussed. Opposing views can then be reconciled on rational grounds and a balance can be achieved which is acceptable to the majority.

Recent considerations of policing policies and police powers appear to be more concerned with balance rather than compromise. The Royal Commission on Criminal Procedure described the concept of a *'fundamental balance'*[22] and posed the question whether there could be, in any strict sense, an equation drawn between the individual on one side and society on the other. They also suggested that the concept of balance might be some sort of contract between the individual and society.[23]

Lord Scarman offered *'consent and balance'* as a basic principle of policing but narrows the wider concept of balance to the particular issue of law enforcement and its effect on public order. He described the basic police function as being the prevention of crime, the protection of life and property and the maintenance of order and emphasised that if the police are to secure the assent of the community which they need to support their operations, they must strike an acceptable balance between the three elements of their function.[24]

The Police Complaints Board, in reviewing the procedure for investigating complaints against the police, were similarly weighing the considerations of accountability to the public and the need to protect the interests of police officers who, by the nature of their office, often attracted ill-founded or malicious allegations. They emphasised that a police officer who is accused has the same right to the presumption of innocence as anyone else. 'We see it as our duty so to exercise our powers as to hold a fair *balance* between the police and the community so far as that is practicable in individual cases.'[25]

This tendency to approach any issue as a matter of balance glosses over those ingredients which maintain the balance between the police on one side and the public on the other. The principle that the police and the public have a local and collective responsibility for preventing crime and maintaining order provides the basis for a balanced approach to policing. This joint responsibility, together with the consent of the public to the existence and authority of the police, is balanced against a system of policing which is characterised by its fairness, reasonableness, openness and integrity. These are the hallmarks of police professionalism which elevate policing from being merely a regulatory and coercive function to a service supported by high ideals and which is supportive of society itself.

The police historian, Charles Reith, has pointed out the contribution which the modern police service has made to the nature of British society and way of life. He points out that history has shown that the absence of restraint by an effective police results in an increase of illegal and criminal activity. He states that, 'police of the kind we have succeeded in evolving in this country are a primary essential of moral welfare and progress. A moral basis for its police is as essential for the welfare and existence of a community as is a moral basis for its law'.[26]

The emphasis I have placed on ethics, discretion and sensitivity is a reflection of the fairness, reasonableness, openness and integrity which are essential factors in weighing police performance against the public expectation of the police role. Any conduct which fails to meet public expectation will invariably result in individual hostility and general concern which increases in proportion to the degree of abuse.

The police cannot afford to lose the trust and confidence of the public and there must be a greater appreciation of what I would call the 'trusteeship of policing' in which the police are the trustees and the public or society are the beneficiaries. The office of a trustee is an onerous one and carries with it important duties and powers. A trustee is required to observe the highest standards of integrity and to be efficient in the management of the affairs of the trust. At the same time, he is subjected to onerous personal liability if he falls below the expected standards of conduct.[27]

If the analogy is pursued further, there is also a similarity between a police officer's duties and powers and those of a trustee since the duties are obligatory and the powers are discretionary. Consequently, duties have to be discharged but a trustee is not required to exercise his powers in a particular manner or even to exercise them at all.

A further significant aspect of the analogy is that there is no general principle that a trustee should consult the beneficiaries although the latter have certain rights. In practice, consultation frequently takes place and occasionally there is a statutory obligation on a trustee to consult the beneficiaries. The wishes of the beneficiaries are not mandatory and the over-riding consideration is the welfare of the trust. This analogy brings Lord Scarman's statutory duty to consult into sharp focus and it tends to support the view that a statutory duty to consult is rarely required.[28] His reminder to police authorities that they were under a duty to exercise their existing powers recognised that these discretionary *powers* should be strengthened by a statutory *duty*.[29]

In dealing with the question of independence and accountability, it is interesting to note that a trustee cannot be compelled to give reasons in connection with the exercise of a discretionary power. The fiduciary nature of the relationship between the police and the public is also supported by the rule that the beneficiaries cannot control the manner in which a trustee exercises his powers. The duty on trustees to maintain equality between the beneficiaries can be compared with the impartiality of the police and there is an interesting similarity between the independence of the police and the principle that a beneficiary cannot control a trustee, the essential point being that he would then be able to exercise the discretionary powers in his own favour.

This simple comparison between the police function and the operation of a trust emphasises the fiduciary nature of policing and that officers hold their office on trust. It is self-evident from the oath sworn on appointment which refers to an officer discharging all duties faithfully according to law. The analogy also recognises that both functions are subject to judicial review if there is a breach of trust or action is taken against the interests of the beneficiaries.

The principles of policing are so essential to the fiduciary relationship between the police and the public that it is important that a conscious effort is made to apply them to all aspects of the police role. These principles are not confined to operational matters and should be reflected in matters such as recruiting, training and selection for promotion. They require continual reinforcement as opportunities arise and they will invariably provide the justification for decisions and directives on policy matters.

There is little doubt that Lord Scarman's Report and the lengthy debate which followed its publication will be seen as an important phase of police history. Previous chapters have contained many extracts from the report which relate to specific principles of policing. These indicate the extent to which the issues raised affect the very nature and structure of modern policing and the way it must adapt to the changes in society. A cautionary note should be added since Lord Scarman's criticisms and comments were directed at the Metropolitan Police. This is not to say that they have no relevance elsewhere since questions of principle are of universal application but it is important that Lord Scarman's Report is seen in perspective and as being primarily concerned with policing in the inner-city areas.

It is only right that the police generally should come under public scrutiny since its healthy state relies on an independent examination and diagnosis. A self-examination may indicate symptoms of ill-health and inefficiency but an objective view may reveal other signs of ill-health which require remedial measures. Policing generally has adjusted to the criticisms of Lord Scarman but there are some who maintain that it was in the inner cities that the 'illness' was diagnosed and that it was inappropriate that all forces should have been offered the prescribed treatment. Nevertheless, the Scarman Report was a healthy reminder that the police must continually monitor changing social conditions and ensure that policies and practices are adjusted as necessary.

The application of traditional principles to such policies and practices will ensure that the police service is able to resist the clamour for reform and the aspirations of politicians. One of the main purposes in writing this book has been to increase public understanding of the origins of the police profession and the principles which have moulded the modern police service. It is important that the public understand the true nature of policing and that a noble tradition of public duty and service should not be undermined by ignoble criticism. The police, themselves, recognise that they must remain faithful to this tradition and ensure that the principles of policing are applied to every aspect of the police function. An awareness of the 'trusteeship of policing' should ensure that traditional values are not lost and that the true freedom of the individual in a democracy is preserved.

POSTSCRIPT

The Changing Scene – from Scarman to Scargill

This postscript has been prompted by the unprecedented scenes of industrial violence which, during 1984, dominated the dispute between the National Coal Board and the National Union of Mineworkers. The Union, under the presidency of Mr. Scargill, posed an open threat to law and order. Extraordinary measures were required to uphold the rule of law and the public witnessed a large-scale police operation, involving officers from forces all over the country, who were required to contain the threat of intimidation and violence.

Whatever the relative merits of the dispute, police officers recognised the need to uphold individual freedom: the freedom to work and the freedom from intimidation. The over-riding principle is that freedom can only exist under the law. The function of the police has always been to preserve public order and to protect individuals against violence.

The police operation, portrayed predictably by critics as an exercise orchestrated by central government, was based on mutual-aid arrangements under the Police Act 1964, which places the responsibility for seeking mutual aid on the local chief officer of police. These mutual-aid arrangements were co-ordinated nationally but the local decisions reflect the principles of local responsibility for law and order and the operational independence of chief officers. Police action met with public approval and the police were conscious of the community problems arising locally after the dispute ended.

The determined intimidation by mass picketing required firm measures by the police who showed great restraint in the face of extreme provocation. The principle of minimum force was much in evidence and it is significant that traditional measures were relied on. The principles of policing were applied to a difficult task and it emphasised the responsibility on the police to maintain law and order in a manner which attracts public approval.

Notes

CHAPTER 1   THE SEARCH FOR PRINCIPLES

1. (Latin) Against the peace of the Lord (King).
2. The function of preserving law and order; the 'peace' is the normal state of civilised life, with an absence of violence or other disturbance.
3. *Tything* or *tithing* – a company of ten households in the Anglo-Saxon system of Frankpledge.
4. *Hundred* – A sub-division of a county or shire, originally based on ten tythings, having its own court.
5. *Shire* – Historically, an administrative district, consisting of a group of hundreds or wapentakes, ruled jointly by an ealdorman and *shire-reeve*, who presided in the shire-moot (court). The word 'shire' is still retained as the terminal element in the name of some English counties.
6. *Shire-reeve* – The ruler of a shire, representing the authority of the King. Origin of *sheriff*, an office still held in English counties, being the chief executive officer of the Crown and having chiefly ceremonial duties.
7. (Latin) Officer in charge of the stables.
8. *Headborough* – The chief man of a tything, also referred to as a *tythingman*. Later became known as a parish peace-officer or petty constable.
9. Abbreviated from *mobile vulgus* (Latin) – the fickle populace.
10. A further comment on the contribution by the Fielding brothers can be found in Chapter 7, 'The Principle of Prevention', on pp. 133–5.
11. P. Colquhoun, *A Treatise on the Police of the Metropolis*, 7th edn, (1806) Preface.
12. Further aspects of Colquhoun's theories are explored in Chapter 7, 'The Principle of Prevention', on pp. 135–8.
13. Colquhoun, *Police of the Metropolis*, p. 2.
14. Ibid., p. 562.
15. P. Colquhoun, *A Treatise on the Commerce and Police of the River Thames* (1800) p. 24.
16. Radzinowicz, *A History of English Criminal Law*, vol. 3, p. 349.
17. Colquhoun, *Police of the River Thames*, p. 38.
18. See, for example, Critchley, *A History of Police in England and Wales* (Constable, 1967).
19. Jeremy Bentham; (1748–1831); English philosopher and jurist; a founder of utilitarianism, an ethical theory which finds the basis for moral distinctions in the utility of actions, i.e., their ability to produce the greatest good for the greatest numbers.
20. *Report of the Select Committee on the Police of the Metropolis*, 17 June 1822 (440).

21. This statement of principle is still included in the present instructions to officers in the Metropolian Police. It is discussed fully in Chapter 7, 'The Principle of Prevention'.
22. A doctrine of constitutional law, attributed to Locke, in his *Second Treatise of Civil Government*, chs 12–13. Theory elaborated by Montesquieu in his *L'Esprit des Lois*, ch. XI, pp. 3–6. '. . . constant experience shows us that every man invested with power is liable to abuse it. . . . To prevent this abuse, it is necessary from the nature of things that one power should be a check on another. . . . When the legislative and executive powers are united in the same person or body . . . there can be no liberty. . . . Again, there is no liberty if the judicial power is not separated from the legislative and the executive'.
23. See comments on p. 13 summarising the conclusions of the Royal Commission on the Police (1836) on the role of the justices.
24. See Chapter 7, 'The Principle of Prevention', pp. 151–2.
25. *Royal Commission on the Police*, Cmnd 3297 (HMSO, 1929) para. 300.
26. *Royal Commission on the Police*, Cmnd 1728 (HMSO, 1962) para. 338.
27. *The Brixton Disorders 10–12 April 1981*, Cmnd 8427, para. 4.55.

CHAPTER 2   BRIXTON – A RE-STATEMENT OF PRINCIPLES

1. *The Brixton Disorders 10–12 April 1981*, Cmnd 8427 (HMSO).
2. Ibid., para. 1.3.
3. Ibid., paras 4.47–4.54.
4. See Chapter 6, 'Principle of Minimum Force'.
5. *The Brixton Disorders*, op. cit., para. 4.64.
6. Ibid., para. 4.67.
7. See Chapter 8, 'Independence and Accountability'.
8. *The Brixton Disorders*, op. cit., para. 4.68.
9. Ibid., para. 4.68.
10. Ibid., para. 4.51.
11. See Chapter 4, 'Police Discretion'.
12. *The Brixton Disorders*, op. cit., para. 4.72.
13. Ibid., para. 4.73.
14. Ibid., para. 4.74.
15. Ibid., para. 4.74.
16. Ibid., para. 4.77.
17. Ibid., para. 4.78. The view that a different approach involving a variation in tactics and greater public co-operation should be the long-term strategy was supported by a subsequent reduction in street robberies (muggings) at Brixton of 39% in the first six months of 1983. The displacement theory was also proved by an increase of 16% in street robberies at Streatham during the same period.
18. Ibid., para. 3.26.
19. Ibid., para. 3.27.
20. Ibid., para. 3.27.

21. Ibid., para. 3.40.
22. Ibid., para. 3.74.
23. Ibid., para. 3.110, at (1) and (7).
24. Ibid., para. 4.90.
25. Ibid., para. 4.90.
26. Ibid., para. 5.72(i).
27. Ibid., para. 4.56.
28. 'Let justice be done, though the heavens collapse' (translation from Lord Scarman's Report).
29. *The Brixton Disorders*, op. cit., para. 4.57.
30. Ibid., para. 4.58. See also Chapter 4, 'Police Discretion'.
31. Ibid., para. 4.58.
32. Ibid., para. 4.33.
33. Evidence of Chief Constable of Greater Manchester to Lord Scarman, op. cit., para. 5.76.
34. Address to 7th Commonwealth Law Conference, Hong Kong, September 1983.

CHAPTER 3   POLICE ETHICS

1. *The Brixton Disorders 10–12 April 1981*, Cmnd 8427 (HMSO).
2. See Chapter 1, note 19.
3. A. V. Dicey, *Law and Public Opinion in England* (1914) p. 121.
4. J. Bentham, *Principles of Penal Law*, p. 368.
5. Ibid., p. 576.
6. Aristotle, *Nichomachean Ethics*, Book 5, chs 1–3.
7. Benn and Peters, *Social Principles and the Democratic State*, ch. 5, 'Justice and Equality'.
8. Ibid., ch. 13.
9. Colquhoun, *A Treatise on the Police of the Metropolis*, 7th edn, p. 600.
10. A good account of Bruce Smith's contribution to American police reform can be found in Patterson Smith, *Pioneers of Policing*, (1977) ch. 11 (T. A. Reppetto).
11. B. Smith, *A Preface to Law Enforcement*, Annals 291 (Jan. 1954): 3.
12. Section 48(1).
13. From the Latin, 'Nullus liber homo capiatur vel imprisonetur aut disseisietur aut utlagetur aut aliquo modo destruatur, nec super eum ibimus, nec super eum mittemus, nisi per legale judicum parium suorum, vel per legem terre.'
14. (Latin) Have (bring) the body (before the court).
15. See Dicey, *Law of the Constitution*, 10th edn, pp. 188–203.
16. (1947) AC 573.
17. *Rice* v. *Connelly* (1966) 2 QB 414.
18. *Donnelly* v. *Jackman* (1970) 1 WLR 562.
19. *Report of the Royal Commission on Criminal Procedure*, Cmnd 8092, para. 1.21.
20. Ibid., para. 1.2.
21. Ibid., para. 1.11.

22. Ibid., para. 1.12.
23. 384 US 436 (1966).
24. *R* v. *Warickshall* (1783).
25. *R* v. *Sang* (1979) 2 AER 1222.
26. Ibid., p. 1230.
27. An Associate Chief Justice of the US Supreme Court (1902–32).
28. *Royal Commission on Criminal Procedure*, op. cit., para. 4.126.
29. Ibid., para. 4.126. (Quoting AULR 14.1, pp. 11–12 and 23.)
30. Ibid., para. 4.123.
31. Ibid., para. 4.130.
32. Ibid., para. 4.130.
33. Ibid., para. 3.68.
34. Ibid., para. 3.68.
35. Ibid., para. 5.1.
36. Ibid., para. 5.4.
37. Ibid., para. 5.5.
38. Ibid., para. 5.6.
39. Ibid., para. 5.7.
40. Ibid., para. 5.8.
41. Ibid., para. 5.9.
42. Ibid., para. 5.10.
43. Council of Europe, Document 4212, 15 January 1979.
44. Ibid., Article 1.
45. Ibid., Article 2.
46. Ibid., Article 3.
47. Ibid., Articles 4, 5 and 7.
48. Ibid., Article 8.
49. Ibid., Article 12.
50. Ibid., Article 13.
51. Ibid., Article 14.
52. Ibid., Article 15.
53. Ibid., Article 16.
54. These conclusions were drawn by the author when lecturing to police officers. They were given a series of situations in which there were increasing degrees of dishonesty and they were asked to give an anonymous response to (a) whether they would be dishonest in such circumstances and (b) whether they thought other police officers were dishonest in the same circumstances. There was a clear pattern that they regarded their own conduct as conforming to a higher standard than that of other police officers.

CHAPTER 4   POLICE DISCRETION

1. See Chapter 8.
2. *The Brixton Disorders 10–12 April 1981*, Report by Lord Scarman, Cmnd 8427, para. 4.58.
3. Extract from Sir Charles Haughton Rafter's introduction to *Moriarty's Police Law* (1929).

4. *The Brixton Disorders*, op. cit., para. 5.76.
5. See Chapter 7.
6. An interesting and informative account of factors affecting an officer's discretion can be found in M. C. Dix and A. D. Layzell, *Road Users and the Police* (Croom Helm/The Police Foundation, 1983) ch. 5.
7. *The Brixton Disorders*, op. cit., para. 4.74.
8. Ibid., para. 4.78. See also ch. 2, note 17.
9. Ibid., para. 4.73.
10. Ibid., para. 8.39.
11. *Report of the Committee on Homosexual Offences and Prostitution* (The Wolfenden Report), (HMSO, 1957).
12. Thurman Arnold, *Symbols of Government*, 160 (1935).
13. Finckenaur, *Journal of Criminal Justice* (US) vol. 4 (1976).
14. *R* v. *Metropolitan Police Commissioner ex parte Blackburn* (1968) 2 WLR 893.
15. Ibid., at p. 902.
16. (1968) 2 WLR 910 per Edmund Davies LJ.
17. *R* v. *Metropolitan Police Commissioner ex parte Blackburn*, 1973 QB 241. See Lord Denning MR, p. 254 and Phillimore LJ, p. 257.
18. Lord Lane, House of Lords, 23 March 1982.
19. See Finckenaur, op. cit., note 13 above.
20. J. Goldstein, 'Police Discretion Not to Invoke the Criminal Process', *Yale Law Journal*, 69, 4.
21. *Shaaban Bin Hussein* v. *Chong Fook Kam* (1969) 3 AER 1626.
22. See Eldridge, 'Modern Tort Problems' (1931), 45, *Harvard Law Review*, 125–6, pp. 1–24 at p. 3.
23. *Report of Advisory Committee on Drug Dependence on Powers of Arrest and Search in relation to Drug Offences*, (HMSO, 1970).
24. *Report of the Royal Commission on Criminal Procedure*, Cmnd 8092, para. 3.25.
25. Ibid., para. 5.4.
26. Ibid., para. 3.69.
27. Ibid., para. 3.72.
28. Ibid., para. 3.76.
29. Ibid., para. 3.77.
30. Ibid., para. 3.77.
31. K. C. Davis, *Discretionary Justice* (1969) ch. IV.
32. Ibid., p. 98.
33. J. Bentham, *Judicial Evidence* (1827) 524.
34. L. D. Brandeis, *Other People's Money* (1933) p. 62.
35. K. C. Davis, 'An Approach to Legal Control of the Police', *Texas Law Review*, vol. 52.
36. A. K. Bottomley, *Criminology in Focus* (Oxford: Martin Robertson, 1979) p. 93.
37. Ibid., p. 94.
38. Following recommendations by the Police Training Council in August 1983, the social and ethical basis of a police officer's role is now included as a broad objective of police probationer training.
39. Magistrates' Courts Act 1980, Section 43(1).
40. Ibid., Section 43(3).
41. *Royal Commission on Criminal Procedure*, op. cit., para. 3.76.

42. Ibid., para. 3.69.
43. Ibid., para. 6.60.
44. Ibid., para. 6.28.
45. A. K. Bottomley, op. cit., p. 99.
46. *Royal Commission on Criminal Procedure*, op. cit., para. 6.29.
47. Ibid., para. 7.12.
48. Ibïd., para. 7.6.
49. District or Prosecuting Attorney in the United States; Procurator Fiscal in Scotland.
50. *Royal Commission on Criminal Procedure*, op. cit., para. 6.38.
51. Ibid. para. 7.10.
52. Ibid., para. 7.7.
53. Ibid., para. 7.59.
54. See note 15 above.
55. Ibid., para. 8.10.
56. Ibid., para. 8.7.
57. Ibid., para. 8.9.
58. See, for example, H. L. A. Hart's *Concept of Law* (Clarendon Press, 1961) pp. 132–4.
59. Neiderhoffer, A., *Behind the Shield: the Police in Urban Society* (NY: Anchor Books, 1969) p. 64.

CHAPTER 5   SENSE AND SENSITIVITY

1. *The Brixton Disorders 10–12 April 1981*, Report by Lord Scarman, Cmnd 8427, para. 5.76.
2. Ibid., para. 5.76.
3. Ibid., para. 4.70.
4. *Police Complaints Board Triennial Review Report 1983*, Cmnd 8853, para. 4.15.
5. Ibid., para. 4.17.
6. M. C. Dix and A. D. Layzell, *Road Users and the Police* (Croom Helm/The Police Foundation, 1983) p. 135.
7. *The Brixton Disorders*, op. cit., paras 3.20–3.21.
8. Dr R. T. Flint. *Psychology of Victims*.
9. Research indicates that there is scope for the police to improve their service to victims. Police inaction was a source of complaint which suggested a need for the police to explain more clearly why little can be done and to provide victims with realistic expectations. M. Hough and P. Mayhew *The British Crime Survey*, Home Office Research Study no. 76, (HMSO, 1983).
10. See *The British Crime Survey*, op. cit., where research has shown that the elderly were the group least likely to be victims of violent crime. Burglary and 'street crime' caused most concern and 60% of elderly women living in inner city areas said that they felt 'very unsafe' when out on foot after dark.
11. *The Brixton Disorders*, op. cit., para. 5.45.

CHAPTER 6 THE PRINCIPLE OF MINIMUM FORCE

1. See historical account in Chapter 1 and Chapter 7.
2. Section 3(1).
3. Section 2(6).
4. See comments in Chapter 4.
5. *Swales* v. *Cox* (1981) 1 AER 1115.
6. Section 2(6).
7. (1981) 1 AER, p. 1119.
8. Ibid., p. 1119.
9. C. Reith, *A New Study of Police History* (1956) p. 287.
10. *Report of the Royal Commission on Criminal Procedure*, Cmnd 8092, para. 3.2.
11. Ibid., para. 3.4.
12. Ibid., para. 3.5.
13. Ibid., para. 3.6.
14. Ibid., paras 3.7–3.8.
15. Ibid., para. 3.9.
16. Ibid., para. 3.135.
17. Ibid., para. 3.137.
18. *The Brixton Disorders 10–12 April 1981*, Cmnd 8427, para. 4.75.
19. Ibid., para. 4.51.
20. Ibid., para. 4.49.
21. See Chapter 4.
22. C. Reith. *Police Principles and the Problem of War* (1940) p. 58.
23. *The Brixton Disorders*, op. cit., para. 4.52.
24. Ibid., para. 4.82.
25. Ibid., para. 4.83.
26. Ibid., para. 4.83.
27. Ibid., para. 5.73.
28. Home Secretary's address to the Police Federation, May 1981.
29. *The Brixton Disorders*, op. cit., para. 5.74.
30. Ibid., para. 5.74.
31. T. A. Critchley.
32. Home Secretary's address to the Superintendents' Association, September 1980.
33. B. Smith, *Police Systems in the United States* (1940) p. 27.
34. Based on figures issued by the National Center for Health Statistics (NCHS) for period 1965–80.
35. See 5th and 14th Amendments to the Constitution (US).
36. See *Meistinsky* v *New York* (1955) 285 Appellete Division 1153.
37. Statement by Mr. R. Kilroy-Silk MP (Ormskirk, Labour) in House of Commons, 16 January 1983.
38. *The Times*, 7 April 1983.

CHAPTER 7   THE PRINCIPLE OF PREVENTION

1. See Chapter 1, 'The Search for Principles'.
2. Preface to '*Enquiry into the Causes of the Late Increase in Robbers, Etc.*' (1751) Works, vol. 7, p. 159 (ed. by Stephen 1882).
3. See, for example, '*Report of the Committee of the House of Commons on Sir John Fielding's Plan, Etc.*', Parliamentary History (1765–1771) vol. 16 (10 April 1770) cols 929–43.
4. '*A Charge Delivered to the Grand Jury, Etc.*' (1766) p. 13.
5. '*History of English Criminal Law*', L. Radzinowicz, vol. 3, pp. 54–62.
6. See Chapter 1.
7. '*A Treatise on the Police of the Metropolis, Etc.*' (1796).
8. Ibid., p. 479.
9. '*A Treatise on Indigence*' (1806) pp. 7–8.
10. Ibid., p. 8.
11. Ibid., pp. 48–9.
12. Ibid., p. 234.
13. See Chapter 1.
14. '*A Treatise on Police*' (6th edn 1800) p. 562.
15. Ibid., p. 561.
16. '*A Treatise on the Functions and Duties of a Constable, Etc.*' (1803), Appendix no. 1, pp. 79–83.
17. '*A General View of the National Police System, Etc.*' (1799) pp. 6–7.
18. '*A Treatise on Indigence*' (1806) p. 78.
19. Criminal Attempts Act 1981, Section 8.
20. See Chapter 1.
21. Memorandum 'To the Chairman of the Committee appointed by the House of Commons to enquire into the present state of the Police of the Metropolis' (1828) p. 2.
22. Sir Charles Reith, '*A New Study of Police History*' (1956) p. 135.
23. *Final Report of the Royal Commission on the Police 1962*, Cmnd 1728, para. 59.
24. Ibid., para. 57.
25. *The Brixton Disorders 10–12 April 1981*, Cmnd 8427.
26. Ibid., para. 4.57.
27. Ibid., para. 4.57.
28. Ibid., para. 4.58.
29. Ibid., para. 4.11.
30. See, for example, Public Order Act 1936, Section 5.
31. *The Brixton Disorders*, op. cit., para. 3.75.
32. See Chapter 8, 'Independence and Accountability'.
33. Public Order Act 1936, Section 3(1).
34. *The Brixton Disorders*, op. cit., para. 7.42.
35. Public Order Act 1936, Section 3(2).
36. Green Paper '*Review of the Public Order Act 1936 and Related Legislation*', Cmnd 7891.
37. The unprecedented scenes of violence involving pickets and police during the miners' dispute in 1984 demonstrate that special measures may be required where there is a clear and open threat to the rule of law.

38. See, for example, Public Order Act 1936, Section 5.
39. See, for example, Metropolitan Police Act 1839, Section 66.
40. *Report of the Royal Commission on Criminal Procedure* (1981), Cmnd 8092, para. 3.14.
41. Ibid., para. 3.21.
42. Ibid., para. 3.23.
43. Repealed as obsolete by the Criminal Law Act 1967.
44. *The Brixton Disorders*, op. cit., para. 7.34.
45. See note 18.
46. Vagrancy Act 1824, Section 4, as amended by Criminal Law Act 1967.
47. Criminal Attempts Act 1981, Section 8.
48. *The Brixton Disorders*, op. cit., para. 7.4.
49. William Cobbett (1762–1835) – a political journalist who campaigned for social and economic reform.
50. *The Brixton Disorders*, op. cit., para. 7.5.
51. Ibid., para. 4.78.
52. J. Alderson, *Policing Freedom* (McDonald Evans) p. 38.
53. *The Brixton Disorders*, op. cit., para. 9.2.
54. J. Alderson, op. cit., pp. 39–41.
55. *Report of H.M. Chief Inspector of Constabulary 1981* (HMSO) 463, para. 1.11.
56. Ibid., para. 7.14.
57. Ibid., para. 1.10.

CHAPTER 8 INDEPENDENCE AND ACCOUNTABILITY

1. *The Brixton Disorders 10–12 April 1981*, Cmnd 8427, para. 4.59.
2. *Royal Commission on the Police 1962*, Cmnd 1728.
3. Ibid., para. 61.
4. Ibid., para. 68.
5. Ibid., para. 72.
6. Ibid., para. 84.
7. The Police Act 1964 and its effect is discussed in Chapter 1, p. 21.
8. See comments of Lord Denning in *R* v. *Metropolitan Police Commissioner ex parte Blackburn* (1968) in Chapter 4.
9. Police Act 1964, Section 48(1).
10. Ibid., Section 50.
11. G. Marshall, *The Government of the Police Since 1964* in *The Police We Deserve*, Alderson & Stead, 1973, p. 60.
12. See pp. 158–9.
13. See note 8 above.
14. Report of the Royal Commission on Criminal Procedure (HMSO) Cmnd 8092, para. 7.15.
15. Police Act 1964, Section 49(3).
16. *Report of the Royal Commission on Criminal Procedure*, Cmnd 8092–1, *Law and Procedure*, para. 161.
17. *Police Complaints Board Triennial Review 1980*, Cmnd 7966, para. 45.
18. Ibid., para. 62.

19. Ibid., para. 45.
20. *The Brixton Disorders*, op. cit., para. 7.17.
21. A rule that provides that a police officer should not be liable to be proceeded against both in respect of a criminal offence and for a like offence under the discipline code in respect of the same events.
22. House of Commons, 25 November 1981.
23. *Police Complaints Procedures*, Cmnd 8681.
24. Ibid., para. 4.
25. Ibid., para. 4.
26. See *Police Complaints and Discipline Procedures*, (HMSO) Cmnd 9072.
27. See Chapter 4, 'Police Discretion'.
28. *The Brixton Disorders*, op. cit., para. 5.56.
29. Ibid., para. 4.73.
30. Ibid., para. 5.57.
31. See p. 21.
32. Police Act 1964, Section 12(2).
33. *The Brixton Disorders*, op. cit., para. 5.62.
34. See Chapter 7, 'The Principle of Prevention', p. 153.
35. See Chapter 2, 'Brixton – a Re-Statement of Principle', p. 28.
36. *The Brixton Disorders*, op. cit., para. 5.70.
37. H.O. Circular 54/1982 of the 16 June 1982.
38. Police Regulations 1979, Regulation 11 and Schedule 2, para. 1.
39. Chief Constable of Greater Manchester, press statement of 15 March 1982.
40. *Report of the Commissioner of the Metropolis for the Year 1982* (HMSO) Cmnd 8928, pp. 3–4.
41. Professor P. J. Stead, Newsam Lecture. Police Staff College, Bramshill. July 1980.

CHAPTER 9   THE APPLICATION OF PRINCIPLES

1. See, for example, C. Reith's *New Study of Police History* (1956) and J. Alderson's *The Principles and Practice of the British Police* in *The Police We Deserve* (1973).
2. *The Brixton Disorders 10–12 April 1981*, Cmnd 8427, para. 8.19.
3. See Mrs Hart's *The British Police* (1951) p. v.
4. *Royal Commission on the Police 1962*, Cmnd 1728, Memorandum of Dissent, paras 12–28.
5. Ibid., para. 16.
6. Ibid., para. 25.
7. Ibid., para. 29.
8. Ibid., para. 26.
9. Police Training Council Working Party's Report on *Community and Race Relations Training For The Police*, February 1983, para. 2.3.
10. Ibid., para. 2.4.
11. Ibid., para. 34.
12. P. Southgate, *Police Probationer Training in Race Relations*, (H.O. Research & Planning Unit, 1982).

13. See Chapter 3.
14. C. Reith, *A New Study of Police History* (1956) p. 288.
15. *The Brixton Disorders*, op. cit., para. 5.51.
16. Ibid., para. 5.35.
17. Ibid., para. 8.30.
18. Ibid., para. 5.18.
19. Ibid., para. 5.3.
20. Ibid., paras 7.9–7.10.
21. *Royal Commission on the Police 1962*, Cmnd 1728, para. 24.
22. *Royal Commission on Criminal Procedure*, Cmnd 8092, para. 1.11.
23. Ibid., para. 1.12.
24. *The Brixton Disorders*, op. cit., para. 4.56.
25. Police Complaints Board Triennial Review 1980, para. 118.
26. C. Reith, *A New Study of Police History* (1956) p. 205.
27. This summary of the relationship between a trustee and the beneficiaries is taken from *Hanbury's Modern Equity*, 9th edn, p. 291 *et seq.*
28. See Chapter 8.
29. *The Brixton Disorders*, op. cit., para. 5.62–5.63.

Index